ELLIOT LOVES

ELLIOT LOVES

---

a play by

JULES FEIFFER

GROVE PRESS

New York

Copyright © 1990 by Jules Feiffer

All rights reserved.

A Grove Press Book
Published by Grove Weidenfeld
a division of Wheatland Corporation
841 Broadway
New York, N.Y. 10003-4793

Published in Canada by General Publishing Company, Ltd.

Library of Congress Cataloging-in-Publication Data

Feiffer, Jules.
    Elliot loves: a play/by Jules Feiffer. — 1st ed.
        p.   cm.
    ISBN 0-8021-1096-7.   ISBN 0-8021-3129-8 (pbk.)
    I. Title.
PS3556.E42E4   1988   88-6959
812'.54—dc19   CIP

Designed by Irving Perkins Associates

Manufactured in the United States of America

Printed on acid-free paper

First Edition 1990

1   3   5   7   9   10   8   6   4   2

for Jenny

ELLIOT LOVES

Characters

ELLIOT
JOANNA
VERA
LARRY
PHIL
BOBBY

Scene

The action of the play takes place in the Near North Side of Chicago in the mid-eighties.

ACT 1

SCENE 1

ELLIOT (*downstage front*): I'll never do better. She's good for me. And sweet and vulnerable. A little older than I like them, but she has an innocent, unspoiled quality, even though she's divorced twice and has two kids. She's thirty-five. What I find so important is that she needs me, you know? And she takes my advice! On her children. Even though I myself have never had children. On investments. On—on politics. Women have almost never accepted my advice. Women have always treated me as if I'm dumber than they are and they're making an effort not to embarrass me by showing it. A kind of irritation with me sooner or later enters every relationship I have. As if nothing I do is what they expect in a man. But they make allowances because I try so hard. And I do try. Nothing, I take nothing for granted! I think all the time, What does she want? What would she like? Will this please her? Buying candy or little thoughtful knickknacks to show how imaginative I can be, that I'm not as simple as she thinks. I fight to avoid being pigeonholed. I spend hours of the day with half my mind on what it is she needs from me, trying to understand the side of her she's not exposing and what I can do to make that side trust me. The secret part of her that she doesn't show. How I can win acceptance from that part that no man

5

has ever reached before. I can spend days in the office, on the phone, in conference with clients, consultations, settling problems, and fifty percent of that time I'm off inside myself trying to figure out ways to make her let me in, let me inside to see something in her no one has seen before. For me, that's a proof of worth, my claim on immortality. Because, look, I know I'm not unique in bed; mostly I try to please, and that's still a mystery to me. I mean I've read all the books and tried the therapies and gone away on couples weekends, and I know less now than I ever did about what to do with a woman. Or even if I make it work for both of us, does it make me feel better? If a woman tells me how great I am I think she's exaggerating. But I'm grateful. And if she tells me I'm not doing enough to please her, I want to wring her neck . . . even though I assume it's true. Because shouldn't I get some credit for all the effort I put in? And if she's active, I resent her. And if she's passive, I resent her. And if she's talkative, I resent her. And if she makes jokes or is overly serious or athletic or badly coordinated—it doesn't matter—it's off the mark. Always is. Always. And the distance between what I need and what I'm getting—that distance—the name I give that is "love." Love is not so much an emotion or a feeling. It's the stuff that fills the void between me and a woman. If that stuff isn't there, then all that exists between us is the gap. We talk across it. We go to movies across it. We drink and go to parties and fuck across it. But the gap counts for more than we do. These are activities. Mere activities. The gap has depth! This void, this gap between us, has quality and substance and shape. And this woman and I are more or less clients to the gap. Silhouettes. (*Pause.*)

With the best will in the world, I tend to make women self-conscious, as if they're not—Very desirable women seem not to know how to behave with me. (*Pause.*)

I bring such questions to sex, such a lack of naturalness. I don't think sex is a truly natural act. I mean just old-fashioned, ordinary, run-of-the-mill, missionary-position sex. That's still a risk to me. (*Pause.*)

I don't know what the rules are. I have to admit I liked it better when it was repressed. I could understand fucking in order to defy convention. But fucking only for pleasure! *Only* pleasure! What the hell is that? I don't see the point. I don't believe anybody believes in it. I always knew—my first time I knew—that someday there'd be payback time. I don't mean that AIDS is God's judgment. It's more my mother's judgment.

Sex without guilt is garbage. It has no moral dimension. No metaphysics. You take the forbidden aspect out of sex, it's as erotic as golf. (*Pause.*)

Today, the average gay person is more manly than I am. Probably has more women friends. I don't have women friends. Never have. I was taught that women wouldn't go to bed with men who were friends. And girls like me as a friend. Girls always wanted to befriend me, and I discouraged them. I was taught that Platonic friendships left you sexually suspect, that bad boys made out and nice, kind, unselfish boys didn't. I don't know if I still believe it. I don't know. The battle of the sexes. I was raised on James Thurber, but he doesn't seem to apply anymore. Not since oral sex. (*Pause.*)

You see, I avoid the issue. I begin to talk about love and immediately switch the topic to sex. I don't know how to talk about love. I know how to talk about sex. I may not know what it is, but I can recognize it if I see it. But love escapes me . . . because it's about the gap. If sex is about an object filling a hole, love is about a hole filling a hole. Emptiness occupies emptiness and becomes fullness, becomes consuming, gigantic . . . like growing a third arm. Or rather, having an appendage amputated and having another one, an invisible one, grow in its place, bigger and better but tender to a point of pain. Love exists outside your opinion of it. (*Pause.*)

I love this woman. I love running errands for her, picking up her dry cleaning, totting up her checkbook, doing her income tax. It isn't a one-way street: she likes to cook for me and buy my clothes, go with me to pick out a suit or sweater. She cleans my apartment! What more do I need in bed? And with me performing my services for her, which aren't considered . . . well, quite manly, and with her performing her services for me, which to say the least are prefeminist services, the old-fashioned-girl services . . . with her as the old-fashioned girl and me as the goody-two-shoes boy, both of us behaving counter to acceptable type, we've entered into a compact of delicious, dirty guilt. I find something secretive and lustful in picking up her dry cleaning: the cotton and polyester dresses under the coat of plastic sheeting gleam at me like naked flesh. And when she comes up to my place to Mop and Glow my floors and change the bed sheets, the consequences of that awesome, counterfeminist act lead us into sexual frenzy. This is how we succeed in putting the lifeblood back into sex. (*Pause.*)

And she is very bright, certainly up to the level of my ex-wife, who used to patronize me, or the other women I've gone with—all better read than I, all quite happy to talk about books I never read or movies I know nothing about and could care less. She doesn't do that. That alone would be enough. But it's more than gratitude. And more than housecleaning. It's as much physical as anything else. Dumb stuff. The way she sits on a chair, with her legs tucked under her and her shoes off. The way she walks, high-waisted, a kind of languid, Southern chic. She's from Memphis. Her stare, which is so intense it's often more than I can handle. The way she seems to physically absorb me. (*Pause.*)

And how she likes to say in crowded places that she loves me. She says it anywhere. Out loud in the supermarket. On the bus. In elevators. The way she dresses. Simple, just right, and no nonsense. As if good taste doesn't involve thought. She has a perfect figure for clothes and wears them as naturally as—as—something is there. A trace of something that separates her from the ordinary. (*Pause.*)

If only she didn't say "piece of cake." I don't know where she picked it up, but she says it all the time. I ask her, "How did your day go?" She says, "Piece of cake." She's a real estate broker. "Did you get that co-op off your hands?" I ask her. "No, but don't let it get to you, it's a piece of cake." That's another thing she's always saying: "Don't let it get to you." Or "Don't get upset." Or "Don't get carried away." And she says these things before I am got to, or upset, or carried away. Her assumption that things "get to me," or "upset me," or "carry me away," the impersonal arrogance of that assumption carries me away. And I yell at her: "You're trying to make me look neurotic, but I'm not neurotic. I'm just not as easygoing as you are. You never worry. You leave your children unattended for hours. Or if you get a sitter you accept total strangers. You trust anybody in this city. So when you trust me, what am I to think? That I'm just one of the mob, part of that tribe of hundreds, thousands of people on the make—criminals, perverts, addicts, con men, fakes, incompetents, assholes—whom you alone, of all women walking this land today, trust? Do you understand now why I'm upset?" And she says, "I understand perfectly," and puts her face so close to mine I get cross-eyed. I flush with emotion. And she says, "I love your smile." And the gap between us fills and I realize I'm in love. And then she says, "Don't get carried away," and the gap empties. (*Pause.*)

"Piece of cake," she says in response to remarks that do not, by any stretch of the imagination, call for "piece of cake." "Are you happy?" I ask her. "Piece of cake." "Do you want to go to the movies tomorrow night?" "Piece of cake." "Let's make love." "Piece of cake." "Was it good for you?" "Piece of cake." (*Pause.*)

I must make this clear: on every other level she is extraordinary. I thrill to her looks, her charm, her wonderful way of listening as if I am the most enchanting man she has ever known . . . but then, at the end of my anecdote or my confession, to say "Piece of cake!" makes a mockery out of our relationship. (*Pause.*)

I probably ask too much. Who am I to demand of the only woman in twenty years—in my life!—who treats me as if I'm singular, intelligent even, as if I *count* . . . who am I to make these demands? What are my grounds? Can I say—dare I say?—"Stop saying 'piece of cake' and I will marry you"? Can I say that? She'd think I'm crazy. But I don't feel crazy. I feel obsessed. I believe, to the root of my being, that if she would only change in these infinitesimal ways that I'm sure bother no one else but affect me like a toothache, if she'd only stop telling me not to get upset and carried away, I swear to you on a stack of Bibles that the doubts I harbor about her, that the desire to run away from her followed a minute later by the desire to spend the rest of my life with her, would be, once and for all, resolved. (*Pause.*)

And tomorrow, after six weeks of seeing each other three times a week, Joanna is meeting my friends.

BLACKOUT

SCENE 2

Evening. The lobby of a chic Chicago apartment building on the Near North Side. A mirror, a bench, an elevator.

JOANNA: Tell me again.

ELLIOT: They're just the guys, that's all. Nothing to be afraid of.

JOANNA: Bobby, Phil, and Leo.

ELLIOT: Larry.

JOANNA: Larry's the one who just got divorced. (ELLIOT *nods.*) Piece of cake.

ELLIOT: And Bobby is married to Vera, and Phil is separated.

JOANNA: Larry is the house painter.

ELLIOT: He owns a paint company. He makes the paint, he doesn't paint houses himself. He's a businessman. Optimum Paints.

JOANNA: Don't get upset.

ELLIOT: I'm not upset. They're waiting for us. We're late.

JOANNA: Elliot, it's only eight o'clock. Don't get carried away.

ELLIOT: You're the one who wanted to meet my friends.

JOANNA: Well, don't you think it's just about time?

ELLIOT: I love you, Joanna. (*Pause.*) Look, they already know you. I've done nothing but rave about you to them. You're not going in there as a stranger. They love you. (*Pause.*) What are you thinking?

JOANNA: You look very nice. I'm so glad you picked that suit over the one I wanted. You look radically handsome in it.

ELLIOT: You look good enough to eat.

(*They kiss.*)

JOANNA: Larry is black?

ELLIOT: Bobby is black.

JOANNA: And he has a white girlfriend.

ELLIOT: They split up.

JOANNA: Is he here alone?

ELLIOT: He's here with his wife, Vera. This is their apartment. They live here.

JOANNA: His wife took him back?

ELLIOT: No one's supposed to know about this. I don't know what Vera knows.

JOANNA: She's white?

ELLIOT (*impatient*): Joanna. . . . Black. She's a supervisor at the telephone company.

JOANNA (*memorizing*): House painter . . . telephone company. Who's the accountant then—Larry?

ELLIOT: Phil.

JOANNA: Then what's Larry? Is he the one who hates women?

ELLIOT: He doesn't hate them. He just got out of a lousy marriage.

JOANNA: He did something just awful to her, though?

ELLIOT: It's complicated. . . .

JOANNA: He did something. Don't tell me. Isn't he the one who stole his wife's car when they split up and drove it off a cliff?

ELLIOT: That doesn't mean he hates women.

JOANNA: He hates cars?

ELLIOT: That's funny.

JOANNA: I say something funny and you tell me it's funny. Well, I know it's funny. Don't you think I know, Elliot? Is it always necessary to point it out to me?

ELLIOT: I'm sorry if I do that. Is it really that important, I mean, to discuss this right now?

JOANNA: You don't laugh at my jokes, you identify them. You do not ever laugh at me. It provokes me. I love you anyhow.

ELLIOT: I'm sorry. Don't worry about Larry. He's had a year of therapy since he drove the car off the cliff.

JOANNA: Piece of cake. I've drawn a blank on Phil. Is he the alcoholic?

ELLIOT: Phil may be an alcoholic. He's got it under control.

JOANNA: We all drink too much.

ELLIOT: Try not to drink so much around Phil. I don't mean just you. Me too.

JOANNA: Phil will have to take care of himself. Tonight I have my own problems.

ELLIOT: He's gotten very quiet. You have to get used to Phil.

JOANNA: Does Phil have a girlfriend? First tell me what he does.

ELLIOT: He's the accountant.

JOANNA: And Bobby's the one who works for *Playboy*. He's the one with the black wife, Violet.

ELLIOT: Vera is her name.

JOANNA: She works. She works for . . .

ELLIOT: AT&T.

JOANNA: I was going to say that. I have it together. How do I look?

ELLIOT: You know what I think.

JOANNA: Hair all right?

ELLIOT: Joanna, let's go. Please. I love you.

JOANNA: Don't get carried away.

ELLIOT: I'm not. I'm just a little. . . .

JOANNA: I love your tie. Did I buy that for you? It looks very smart with that shirt. Your friends are going to think I don't live up to you.

ELLIOT (*beams*): I think you look beautiful.

JOANNA: Did you see that story in the *Tribune* this morning? Mayor Sawyer—

ELLIOT: Which story?

JOANNA: I was about to tell you, Elliot.

ELLIOT: Can you tell me upstairs?

JOANNA: Now calm down. Mayor Sawyer was in his limo on his way to a meeting on the North Side, when he spotted an old lady being mugged—are you all right?

ELLIOT: I just think we should get upstairs.

JOANNA: Don't let it get to you. And he got out of his limo—

ELLIOT: Whose limo?

JOANNA: Mayor Sawyer.

ELLIOT: Why are we talking about Mayor Sawyer?

JOANNA: It was a story. I'm telling you this amusing story from today's *Tribune* in order to relax you.

ELLIOT: Can you tell me in the elevator?

JOANNA: For pity's sake, we're going! Don't be rude. May I finish? He breaks up the mugging. And the police come. And they ask him his name. No one knows who he is!

ELLIOT: Wouldn't you say it's rude to be twenty-five minutes late to a dinner?

JOANNA: Elliot, no one, not the old lady, the muggers, the police— no one recognized the Mayor. (*A long exchange of stares.*) Piece of cake. I just want to go over my notes.

ELLIOT: That's also funny—notes.

JOANNA: I'm not joking. (*Scans notes.*)

ELLIOT: What are those? Seriously, Joanna.

JOANNA: Don't get hot and bothered.

ELLIOT: What notes? Let me see!

JOANNA: Now don't let it get to you. It's nothing at all. Just little reminders of what you like to have me talk about: the drugstore story, the Marshall Field story, the day I ran away from the kids.

ELLIOT: Oh, Joanna. . . .

JOANNA: Your friends, Phil and Bobby and Larry, should like these. (*Finishes with notes.*) Okay. I must say, I'm exhausted.

ELLIOT: You're making too much of this.

JOANNA: They'll take to me, won't they, Elliot?

ELLIOT: No, it'll be fine. Fine!

JOANNA: Because if they don't—

ELLIOT: Believe me, Joanna, we may have problems but this is not going to be one of them.

JOANNA: What problems do we have?

ELLIOT: I just mean—

JOANNA: This is a fine time to bring up our problems.

ELLIOT: You're the one who's always telling me, "Don't let it get to you."

JOANNA: This time I believe *you* are the naive one.

ELLIOT: You may be right.

JOANNA: Stop humoring me! You are naive, Elliot. You believe everything I tell you—even when I'm lying—so how can I trust your assurances about your friends?

ELLIOT: You don't lie. About what?

JOANNA: You're not even curious. I take advantage of you, Elliot.

ELLIOT: Please. Not now.

JOANNA: You know when we go out to dinner and I insist that this time it's on me and then I never have enough money and you have to pay?

ELLIOT: It's funny. It's charming. So what?

JOANNA: I have the money. I carry two hundred dollars in my purse at all times. I don't want to spend it. You'll never want to see me again when you hear this: I hate to spend money. I never pay for anything if I can help it, not even when I lunch with my girlfriends. They're onto me. It embarrasses them so that they don't bring it up, but they know very well what a cheap-skate I am. You never guessed?

ELLIOT: You'd pay for me if it was important.

JOANNA: I would never pay for you.

ELLIOT: You don't mean that.

JOANNA: I would rather die than pay for you. (*Pause.*) I will buy things only for my children. Are you upset?

ELLIOT: Joanna, we were supposed to be upstairs half an hour ago. Please, I beg you!

JOANNA: I'd move heaven and earth for my children. I save all my money for my children's future. None of us can be sure about the future. I can't predict mine, much less theirs. I must provide for them.

ELLIOT: I agree. It's perfectly understandable.

JOANNA: You don't know what it means to have children. It doesn't mean I don't love you. How did you get to be so old and not have children? It's very selfish of you, really. How did your wife let you get away with it? Without children, there's no substance to life. I'm sure that's why she left you.

ELLIOT: She left me for another man.

JOANNA: And now she has children.

ELLIOT: I want children, Joanna. I have always wanted children.

JOANNA: If you wanted a child, you'd have one by now!

ELLIOT: I'd want a child with you.

JOANNA: I don't want any more children.

ELLIOT: Then what are we *talking* about?

JOANNA: I'm trying to understand the kind of man you are. Are you truly that selfish? I don't believe you are. What's the answer?

ELLIOT: Look, I love your children. You've said it yourself, how much they like me.

JOANNA: It's easy for you. It's not the same. You're not a real person until you're a parent. You're a shadow. You're one-dimensional.

ELLIOT: How can you talk to me this way? I take care of you. I run errands. I serve you.

JOANNA: Remember, I serve you too. I'd respect you more if you didn't talk about it. I hate you for saying that.

ELLIOT: I can't stand you hating me, Joanna.

JOANNA: Calm down. It's not all that serious.

ELLIOT: How can we go up to my friends with you hating me? You know how late we are? How can you have secrets if you love me?

JOANNA: I don't believe anyone's ever loved you before. I must protect myself.

ELLIOT: This hurts.

JOANNA: Don't be vulnerable with me now, Elliot. It's unkind.

ELLIOT: I know tonight is a strain . . .

JOANNA: —it's going to be a very bad time with us if they don't like me.

ELLIOT: Then the hell with'em!

JOANNA: We will have a hard time surviving it. Believe me. You know these men a lifetime. For example, I have two friends whom you will meet—my two closest friends—

ELLIOT: Joanna—

JOANNA: Walter and Fay Derringer.

ELLIOT: You've told me about them.

JOANNA: Please bear with me. And they are always touching each other, Walter and Fay, in front of me.

ELLIOT: What are you saying? I don't touch you enough?

JOANNA: Don't anticipate me. You touch me just fine. I don't know why, two people when they come together, the rest of the world changes dimension. Is the rest of the world so intolerable that just because you've found one other person, a man you prefer to be with—

ELLIOT: Is this going to take long?

JOANNA: —and when an outsider, a friend, breaks into that equation, for example Fay and I, we have known each other forever. When we're yammering away, I can see, visually see Walter disappearing before my eyes. The way my father did when my mother and her sisters held court. As if a woman diminishes a man if she's not paying full attention. Which is why I'm afraid sometimes because we've been alone, truly alone, and now I'll meet your friends and the next step is you will meet mine and forgive me, Elliot, but I find this just a bit threatening. Is that crazy?

ELLIOT: But sooner or later, Joanna—

JOANNA: I know that! Forgive me, I'm demented. But I do have a point. I know I do. This changes everything.

ELLIOT: We have to meet each other's friends eventually.

JOANNA: I want to meet your family.

ELLIOT: I don't believe this is happening!

JOANNA: What do you want me to do?

ELLIOT: This wasn't my idea.

JOANNA: Let's stand'em up.

ELLIOT: Be reasonable.

JOANNA: I don't want to meet your friends, Elliot.

ELLIOT: What do you want me to do? What am I supposed to do?

JOANNA: I'm not ready. I'm not sure I want to be judged yet.

ELLIOT: It's too late, Joanna.

JOANNA: *You* go on up.

ELLIOT: I'm sorry. This is my fault. I'm sorry. I shouldn't have rushed it. What will I tell them? What can I possibly say?

JOANNA: Don't say anything. Please don't say anything. Please don't tell them anything about me. Come home with me now, Elliot!

ELLIOT: I can't do this, Joanna.

JOANNA: I'm going home. What are you going to do?

(ELLIOT *rings for the elevator. It opens and he steps in. The door closes on him.*)

ELLIOT (*muffled*): It's 22G!

JOANNA (*facing elevator*): Piece of cake.

BLACKOUT

SCENE 3

Evening. The terrace of a high-rise. Upstage, a closed glass door behind which we see shaded figures moving about as at a small party. ELLIOT *stands at the terrace railing, a drink in his hand. He is looking nowhere. The terrace door opens and* VERA, *an attractive black woman in her thirties, steps out. We hear laughter from the party behind her before she closes the door on it.*

VERA: Weatherwise, you have no complaints. The Big Dipper. (*Pause.*) Look, Elliot.

ELLIOT (*doesn't look*): I can't locate the Big Dipper, Vera. I never have.

VERA: That's silly. There's the cup and there's the handle. Don't look at me, look where I'm pointing. Okay?

ELLIOT (*doesn't look*): It's a bunch of stars to me, Vera.

VERA: Oh, you're not even trying.

ELLIOT: I've never understood the big deal about the Big Dipper.

VERA (*laughs*): You're so funny. My seventeen-year-old, Chuckie, he has no curiosity either. I don't understand that. He has no interest whatsoever in going to college.

ELLIOT (*irritated*): Did I say I don't have curiosity? (*Pause.*) I don't think I learned anything in college.

VERA: There had to have been one good teacher, Elliot.

ELLIOT: Don't misunderstand me, I don't blame the teachers. I have a hard time I guess listening.

VERA: Our people have to go to college, Elliot. It's different with you.

ELLIOT: I wasn't interested in school—not for a day, not for a minute.

VERA: You're too intelligent to talk that way.

ELLIOT: Did I say I wasn't intelligent?

VERA: No. I said you're very intelligent. (*Pause.*) Elliot, you're just down on the world tonight. With good reason. You hear what I'm saying to you?

ELLIOT: College prepares you for the wrong things. It doesn't make you educated. It's bull! It's no more or less than a union card. It has nothing to do with the real world.

VERA: But it's useful, it's necessary. You went, I went. You do very well. Would you do as well if you hadn't gone to college?

ELLIOT: Henry Ford didn't go to college. Thomas Edison. (*Pause.*) Lincoln. (*Pause.*) Lawyers weren't required to go to law school before the First World War.

VERA: You wouldn't want a doctor who didn't go to medical school.

ELLIOT: The family doctor, the old family doctor of fifty years ago with half as much education—people thought he was God.

VERA: Ignorant people.

ELLIOT: Everybody!

VERA: What're you telling me? I shouldn't send my black baby to college? What do you want him to do—shine shoes?

ELLIOT: Oh, come on, Vera. Not tonight. Not tonight, please. All I'm saying is there are too many people around who give a college education too much importance. I work with a bunch of jerks, half of them with doctorates. And none of them gets the better of me. Send the kid to a good computer school; colleges are done for. I know what I'm talking about.

VERA: You're just in a bad mood. College gives you the preparation, Elliot. Don't say no. You can't overlook preparation. Okay?

ELLIOT: Shove the preparation!

VERA (*near tears*): Well, you may be ready to throw out the baby with the bath water!

ELLIOT: Oh, listen, I don't mean a word of what I'm saying. You're right, Vera, you don't want to listen to me.

VERA: Sometimes you just go too far. Okay? (*Starts to leave.*) No, I understand. Come in when you feel more like it. (*Exits inside.*)

ELLIOT (*vehement, at stars*): Big fucking Dipper!

(LARRY *and* PHIL, *both in their forties, enter from living room, talking. They talk only to each other, but most of their focus is on* ELLIOT, *whom they are determined to cheer up.*)

PHIL: . . . Well, you can't blame Sinatra for living too long.

LARRY: I can't look at him the way he combs his hair now. Who's he trying to kid? The man's a parody! If he died at forty-five— Maggio, "Songs for Swinging Lovers"—he'd be the stuff of legend instead of what? Some kind of sub-Mafia, Atlantic City joke. Stars who live too long, it's sick!

PHIL: Not James Dean.

LARRY: My point, exactly. Try to imagine a potbellied, baggy-eyed, balding, coke-sniffing Jimmy Dean. Disgusting! Jimmy

Dean at thirty-five, forty-five—impossible. He went at the right time. But Sinatra, or take Brando . . .

PHIL: Take Brando, please!

LARRY: A disgrace! Brando. People live past their own ripeness. It's not age, it's ripeness. Cary Grant. Astaire. They were still ripe in their eighties. But if you want to name names, Presley.

PHIL: Or, say, Joe McCarthy. He died at the right time.

LARRY: But not Nixon. He should have passed over ten minutes after Watergate. But look at him. He wouldn't die if you drove a wooden stake through his heart.

PHIL: He'd take it as a deduction.

LARRY: Paul Newman. He can carry off sixty. A hell of a job, the amount of beer he consumes and all. The man's the cream of the crop. But Tony Curtis? I don't think he's any older than Paul and he looks a hundred.

PHIL: Hard living.

LARRY: Don't give me hard living. Paul races at Le Mans, for Christ's sake. These men are legends; they should know when to stop.

PHIL: Would you know? Would I know?

LARRY: It's not our job to know. We're not living legends, we're living assholes. Nobody notices how we age because everyone who knows us ages at the same rate. But movie stars, politicians—they leave a film record. Jerry Lewis when we were growing up versus Jerry Lewis today. Tell me that's not demoralizing. I look at him on one of these fucking telethons, I feel like pledging two million for him to retire.

PHIL: Mike Wallace—he goes on forever.

LARRY: Ageless. But Sinatra—he was my hero, I worshipped Sinatra. When I came on to girls I came on like I was Sinatra. Why does he do this to me? Let me tell you something: if Jesus lived to be sixty, he wouldn't have a religion named after him. Elliot—look at him. He looks worse than Sinatra.

PHIL: Elliot was born looking old.

LARRY: Because he worries too much. In high school, the worrywart, remember? He was always worried. The worrywart, we called him. Remember?

PHIL: Yeah, I remember. I remember we went ice skating once.

LARRY: Once, sure, once. But what about all the other times when he worried and I *didn't* fall through the ice.

PHIL: He should have let you drown.

LARRY: Look at the price I paid. First he worries I'll fall through the ice; then he worries I'll panic just because I *do* fall through the ice; then he worries that I'll drown him when he jumps in after me; then he worries I'll catch pneumonia after he fishes me out. He was the one sick for three weeks after; I go back to St. George on Monday and play in the finals. Does Elliot play? No, because he's worried himself sick over me, who doesn't catch a sniffle. So I scored twenty-six points in the finals, and for my sins for celebrating when my best friend's in bed with a hundred and four temperature, I score with Delores Donahue at the victory party who nobody, we thought, made out with. And she gives me the clap. Because Elliot, Elliot worried. I made him smile.

(PHIL *looks over at* ELLIOT, *who reluctantly smiles.*)

ELLIOT: Fuck you, Larry.

LARRY: Same to you and many of them. (*Stares at his empty glass.*)

I need another. (*To* PHIL:) You? Come on, one's not going to hurt you.

PHIL: Unh-unh.

LARRY: What have I got on my hands—two worrywarts? I'll be back in a flash, Flash. (*Exits to living room.*)

PHIL: Last time I was out here I peed off the terrace. You can't pee off the terrace sober.

ELLIOT: Larry's got too much energy for his own good.

PHIL: Everyone talks about support groups for alcoholics. You know? Somebody should talk about countersupport groups. "Come on, one little drink won't hurt you." I've never been offered so many drinks in my life since I went on the wagon. The shit you get away with drunk. You know? You can't drop water bags off a terrace sober.

ELLIOT: You never did that.

PHIL: Not here. A couple of years ago. Condoms filled with water. I can't remember the name of the girl I woke up in bed with that night. You know? But I remember the condoms filled with water. That's what I have nostalgia for. The freedom. I'm a tightass sober; I'm a free man drunk. You know? I talked women into bed I wouldn't have the nerve to open my mouth to sober. I made friends. You know? I could never talk up to people the way Larry does. You know? But five or six bourbons, I could tell jokes. I don't know how to tell a joke, but I could tell 'em drunk. You know? I was better at everything drunk . . . except marriage and work. You know? And I prefer drinking to both. I bet JFK could put it away. Bet he could hold his liquor too. I bet he was a couple of sheets to the wind all through the Cuban missile crisis. I know I'd be. Adlai Stevenson and the Joint Chiefs in one room, Judith Exner in the next. You know? Can you imagine me peeing off a balcony with JFK? Teddy maybe, not Jack. Jack was a classy drunk. I'm more like Teddy. Black guys—they really pull out the jams drunk. Hispanics too. They get crazy—you know?—the music and everything. Crazy. They get high on the noise. Not Jews, though. When Jews get drunk they confuse it with their role in the universe. They don't have fun, they have insights. You can just bet that Einstein had a bag on the night he came up with $E=MC^2$.

(ELLIOT *laughs*.)

You think that's funny? You want to put money on Freud being smashed the night he came up with the Oedipus complex?

(ELLIOT *turns away, smiling*.)

Karl Marx—he came up with communism tanked. You know, Elliot? Four in the morning, bombed out of his mind. If he hadn't made notes, he would have forgotten it the next morning and we're all better off. Right? Right. You know? Wasps drunk—Wasps drunk are no different from Wasps sober. You know? Upper-class Wasps, I mean, upper-class. Lower-class—they know how to have a good time. But upper-class Wasps, you know—you know?—they get paranoid drinking that, that they'll lose control. Right? Right. An ex-altar boy like me, you know, I only feel in control when I'm drunk; but Wasps, who really are in control, when they get drunk they get afraid that they'll lose it. You're not smiling. That's okay too. This is the best time I've had since I quit drinking, and it's because you don't care if I'm alive or dead. If you're just holding that glass, Elliot, and not drinking on account of me, you don't have to. I'm past that.

ELLIOT: What?

PHIL: You know? Because it doesn't bother me. Everyone inside is getting smashed. They're upset. They're upset for you.

ELLIOT: Don't rub it in. I guess I rushed things.

PHIL: You? Captain Caution? What are you talking about?

ELLIOT: You think I'm too cautious?

PHIL: What do I know? The thing with old friends, you know, they think it's still high school. You know? I mean how much do we see of each other? When I do your taxes.

ELLIOT: More than that.

PHIL: I'm not complaining. I can do something about it too. I live two blocks away from here, over on State. I see Bobby—a rough guess—five, six times a year. You know what I'm saying? Do I know you now, you know? A little, but mostly I know you from St. George, back when. You covered all bases—you know? You thought two steps ahead of everybody. So we have to give that a name. You know? Because Larry and Bobby and myself—we were less mature than you; maybe a little better athletes, but you were terrifically mature for your age. Like you talked like our parents sometimes—

ELLIOT: Thanks a lot.

PHIL: What can I say? So we called you worrywart and Captain Caution. But what's that got to do with today? You were just good at giving advice. You thought about things; we didn't. But now I think about things too, and I even give advice.

ELLIOT: You got some for me?

PHIL: Sure. This, too, shall pass. (*Pause.*) Your other friends who I don't know anything about, the world of polltakers . . . are they like us?

ELLIOT: I don't have friends from the job.

PHIL: I have two good friends who are accountants, but I don't see them alone. We see each other with our wives.

ELLIOT: There's less horsing around with my other friends. Outside of you guys, I don't have a single friend who I know ten years.

PHIL: Outside of shoptalk and gossip, my friends' wives, you know, they're the ones I talk real to.

ELLIOT: Like?

PHIL: It's hard to say. You know? But I get a lot off my chest.

ELLIOT: Like me with Joanna.

PHIL: Yeah, it's more natural.

(*Long pause, during which* PHIL *looks over at* ELLIOT, *then front again.* BOBBY, *a black man their age, enters from the living room with* VERA.)

VERA: The ladies have come to a decision. You men should be free to hang out, so we gals are going bye-bye for a couple of hours. Okay?

ELLIOT: You don't have to do this, Vera.

VERA: You'll be more relaxed. Okay?

ELLIOT: Where will you go? I can't kick you out of your own apartment.

VERA: Downtown to a movie. Don't worry—okay? It's all arranged, Elliot. We're well taken care of.

ELLIOT: How are you going to get there? Take my car. You don't want to look for a cab, three women downtown after a movie.

VERA: We'll call for a cab—okay? Now, you have enough on your mind.

ELLIOT: You don't want to wait around for a cab late at night, if they show up.

VERA: Don't worry. We're big girls, we can take care of ourselves.

ELLIOT: Vera, really, I'm not going to feel right. What time does the movie let out? Waiting around after midnight for a cab. We'll come down and pick you up. What time does the movie let out?

VERA: We can decide all that later.

ELLIOT: Maybe we all should go.

BOBBY: Relax, man! Nobody's gonna pick on these women. They're too big, they're too old, and they're too mean.

ELLIOT: Vera, I was off base before. Chuckie has to go to college. If he doesn't get on the right track now, who can tell what the job market will be like tomorrow? If you want me to talk to the boy. . . .

VERA: Be good—you hear? (*Exits.*)

ELLIOT: Jesus, Bobby. Hey, Vera! *I'll* go! Hey, Vera!

BLACKOUT

SCENE 4

Bobby's study, fifteen minutes later. A dark, book-lined room, very masculine. On the wall, various athletic trophies and businessman merit awards. An advanced-systems stereo, TV, VCR. Many video cassettes lying around. Copies of Playboy *lie scattered on a small coffee table. Bottles of Chivas and Jim Beam. A fancy phone system. The four friends lounge about, all but* PHIL *drinking heavily.*

BOBBY (*to* LARRY): You shoot off your mouth, but you forget the context.

LARRY: It's PMS, don't shit us, Bobby. (*To* ELLIOT:) I guarantee you, I've lived through this.

BOBBY: What Elliot's talking about is larger than one man, one woman.

LARRY: I don't care what you say, Bobby. (*To* ELLIOT:) You should have seen Angela two days before her period. I don't lie to you: she was a crazy woman. It was a nightmare. She picked fights over anything. Check it out. Premenstrual syndrome. "Good Morning America" did a whole week on it. This is typical. What you don't want, you don't let her get you into an argument on the specifics. Women will kill you on the specifics. That's their turf: detail. "Larry, you said this." "You promised me that." "You didn't come through, Larry." They grind you into the woodwork with detail. I mean, you want to talk pussy-whipped.

ELLIOT: I'm not pussy-whipped.

LARRY: I didn't say you. Me. I'm saying me. Christ, take it easy—
all right? I gave Angela a long rein. You listening to me? A
long rein. Two or three days before her period, I took a hike.
It's fucking hilarious.

BOBBY: What we're discussing is larger than you and Angela: it's
history.

LARRY: Gimme a break, will ya?

BOBBY: It's history, it's cultural anthropology.

LARRY (*with disdain*): You know, ever since you went to work for
Playboy—where's my man, Bobby? Remember how Bobby
convinced us we should order the satin team jackets with our
names in script over the pockets? "Larry." "Elliot." "Bobby."
"Flash." Hey, Phil, you don't like to be called "Flash" anymore. I liked "Flash." Let's take a vote, you guys. Do we call
Phil "Flash" or "Phil"? Raise your hands. (*No one makes a
move.*) I vote for "Flash." Nobody voting with me? Fuck you
all! Bobby, remember we ordered these jackets on your say-so?
You said you'd loan us the money, and it's bullshit! You don't
have the money any more than we do, and Sapperstein comes
after our fathers for three hundred dollars.

BOBBY: My man Larry's got a hard-on for the past. You should be
ashamed of yourself, man, the words you use—"pussy-whip."
Nothing wrong with "pussy-whip." "Pussy-whip" is marriage
in its ideal condition. I am pussy-whipped and I am proud!

LARRY: Gimme a break!

BOBBY: Any man with responsibilities, any man with a family is
pussy-whipped. "Pussy-whip" is on the side of history.

LARRY (*to others*): You believe this? Do you fucking believe this!?
I'm too proud, I'm too proud. Where's your pride, Bobby?

BOBBY: Man, your pride led you to drive your wife's BMW off a
cliff—that's asshole pride. It's antihistorical pride. No way.

What I have is black family pride. That's the pride my people call for now, and for this time and this place I not only have it, I glory in it. Examine your condition, man. The words we use. Single men have what? They have "balls." Then they get married and what do they have? "The family jewels." When you're single, it's not "the family jewels." Oh no. Only with marriage. Single men, they "fool around." Married men "settle down." "Fooling around" is lightweight; "settling down"—that's serious, that's for real, that's significant. These are not careless metaphors. They mean exactly what they say. When a man's balls quit fooling around and settle down and become the family jewels, it's a significant transformation. They are no more my balls, not Phil's balls, not Larry's balls, not Elliot's; our balls become community property. They become socialized. This is what we're talking about—you hear?—the socialization of balls. And tell me, what do you get when you socialize balls? You get "family." That's what we call "family." That's what we call the "future of the race." We are cogs in a vast, historic continuum. Our balls are not our own, Elliot, they are fodder for the future. So if it's not this one, this Joanna woman, it'll be another Joanna, a future Joanna. History doesn't care which Joanna, so long as you line up your balls for the long march. Sooner or later, you've got to get in step, man! (*To* LARRY:) You too!

LARRY: Gimme a break! I don't hear "family" out of you when you show me your dirty pictures, man. Just because you work for *Playboy.* What is this—guilt? You're a fucking hypocrite, Bobby. You want me to believe in "propagation of the species"? Go to work for *Good Housekeeping.* (*To others:*) He's putting us on. The man goes to orgies.

BOBBY: Bullshit.

LARRY: The last time we got drunk—come on, man, the pictures! The pictures! Show these guys the pictures!

BOBBY: I was putting you on.

LARRY: *Now* you're putting me on. You believe in the family; sure, you do . . . until a piece of ass comes along.

BOBBY: I'd be the last to deny that I aim high, and sometimes I do fall.

PHIL: What pictures, Bobby?

BOBBY: Hey, you don't want to see any pictures.

PHIL: How come Larry rates and we don't?

BOBBY (*shrugs*): How you boys do try to corrupt me.

PHIL: I'd like to see the pictures, if there are any pictures. I've got a right to see them.

BOBBY (*shakes his head*): Elliot? Well (*pause*) this is your party.

ELLIOT: What do I care?

BOBBY: There is a good time and a bad time.

ELLIOT: I don't need you to be my nurse, Bobby.

BOBBY (*coldly*): Like the man says.

(*He takes a large envelope off the coffee table and tosses it to* ELLIOT. ELLIOT *hesitates, then takes six ten-by-twelve photos out of the envelope.* LARRY *and* PHIL *bunch up behind him and stare over his shoulder. As he finishes with one photo, he hands it to* LARRY, *who examines it and hands it to* PHIL. *They are quiet for a long while.*)

PHIL: This is not for real.

LARRY (*delighted*): They're dykes!

PHIL: Jesus Christ!

ELLIOT: Were they on drugs?

BOBBY: I don't know what they were on. They were on each other—
I know that.

ELLIOT: They're limber—I'll say that.

PHIL: Fabulous.

LARRY: Fabuloso!

PHIL: I find this hard to believe.

ELLIOT: Two women.

BOBBY: That turns you on?

ELLIOT: They can't be eighteen.

LARRY: What do you want?

ELLIOT: Bobby, do they—they do this—they're both very
beautiful—how do they come to do this?

BOBBY: Yes . . . you could consider this a performance.

PHIL: Christ, look what they're doing here.

BOBBY: A demonstration of sorts.

PHIL: There's nothing, nothing sexier, you know, than two women
doing it! Nothing sexier! Nothing!

(ELLIOT *withdraws.*)

LARRY: God, I'd love to be there!

PHIL: Right in the middle!

BOBBY: Francine and Fredericka. (*Hands* PHIL *a business card.*)

PHIL: They got business cards?

LARRY: No shit? How much?

BOBBY: I can get you the corporate rate. Elliot?

ELLIOT (*feigns interest*): H'yo!

BOBBY: Wouldn't you like to watch these two foxes in action? Take 'em on after?

LARRY: For tonight?

BOBBY: Any night you like.

PHIL: I don't know what it is . . . two women . . . they really know how to do it. They really know—you know? The right places.

LARRY: Now wait a minute, Bobby. This isn't another put-on . . .

PHIL: I mean it's kind of poetic—you know?

BOBBY: Poetry in motion. I also have a cassette.

LARRY: You can get us *these* broads?

ELLIOT (*uneasy*): Come on, you guys . . .

BOBBY: Larry's got the devil in him tonight!

PHIL: Did you say a cassette?

(BOBBY *nods, reaches behind couch, pulls out a cassette and inserts it in the* VCR, *punches it on. All wait for picture.*)

ELLIOT: I don't think I can see this tonight. (*Starts to leave.*)

PHIL: Give it a chance, Elliot! What can you lose? Give it a chance!

BOBBY (*turns off picture*): No.

LARRY: Hey! Hey! Hey! Bobby!

BOBBY: This is Elliot's privilege. He has veto rights.

LARRY (*whines*): Elliot!

PHIL: It doesn't hurt to look, Elliot. Right?

ELLIOT: I don't want to spoil your party. Look, it's a bad night for me. Now I'm spoiling it again. I'll just go.

LARRY: Come on, Elliot!

PHIL: This is *your* party.

ELLIOT: There's no reason my lousy mood should get in the way. You guys have a good time.

PHIL: We're not going to have a good time if you go home.

BOBBY: If he's not in the mood—

PHIL: Hey, I can see this some other time.

ELLIOT: Look, another night there's nothing I'd rather watch.

LARRY: Jesus, Elliot, give us a break, for Pete's sake!

ELLIOT: You want to see it? I'm not stopping you.

LARRY: You are stopping us. You always stop us. It never changes with you. You've always been the one who holds back.

BOBBY: Lay off, Larry.

PHIL: Don't be an asshole, Larry.

LARRY: I don't believe for one fucking moment it's your mood. I mean I'm sorry, I'm sorry, all that crap, all the crap you're going through. But I gotta be honest. I don't think the day will come in our lifetime when you, Elliot, will want to see this film.

BOBBY: Lighten up.

ELLIOT: I don't want an argument, Larry.

LARRY: I'm asking.

ELLIOT: Why is it such a big deal?

BOBBY: Hey, Larry, pour yourself a drink, man. Lighten up.

ELLIOT: I'm sorry. I know I'm wrong, but it does the opposite of
    what it's supposed to. Normally I sit through it. But I can't
    tonight. I'm sorry, I can't. I apologize. It embarrasses me. It
    brings out the lapsed Catholic in me. I wish I could get the
    kicks out of it you guys get. I envy you. I feel lousy about it. I
    don't say I don't like looking. Naked girls, yes . . . as long as
    it's erotic. But pictures of women sticking their fingers up their
    cunts. Dildos. Vibrators. Kiddie porn. I don't like watching a
    blowjob on a TV set. In Vera's house. I'm bothered by it. I'm
    bothered by it. I'm an adult; I know I'm not supposed to be
    bothered. I'm ashamed. I wish I had it in me tonight to do this
    for you.

(*He runs out of words. Others stir uncomfortably.* BOBBY *puts the
photos back in the envelope, takes the cassette out of the* VCR, *and
hides it again behind the couch. Finally,* PHIL *grabs the business
card and crosses to the phone. He dials. All look on as he waits.*)

PHIL: Hello. I'd like to speak to—um— (*Checks card.*) Wrong
    number.

(PHIL *hangs up, looks around helplessly.* ELLIOT *crosses, takes
phone, reads card in* PHIL's *hand, and dials.*)

ELLIOT: Francine? . . . Fredericka! I hope I'm not calling too late,
    my friends and I. My friends would like to make a date . . . I
    don't know, how many can you handle? . . . Well, no, we're
    only four. And you're two—right? Do you think you can
    handle that? . . . Sounds good to me . . . sounds good. . . .
    Yes . . . well, we saw your pictures. . . . Uh-huh. . . . Which
    one are you? The white girl . . . oh, you're the athletic one.
    Both of you? Then this is our lucky night. . . . You are? . . .
    Why, yes, sure, right now.

BOBBY (*alarmed*): What are you saying, man?

ELLIOT: Right, as good a time as any. . . . Say, how much—um, how much do you, do you charge? Well . . . well . . . (*To others:*) It's five hundred for two hours.

BOBBY: Get off the goddamn phone, man!

PHIL: Five hundred? (*To* LARRY:) It's a lot of money.

BOBBY: Hang up! Hang up!

LARRY: Yes! Yes! Go for it!

BOBBY: Goddammit!

PHIL: Five hundred—I don't know, Elliot.

BOBBY: What kind of shit is this!

LARRY (*to* PHIL): Shut up! (*To* ELLIOT:) Absolutely! You can't back down now.

PHIL: Can we call back in a minute?

BOBBY: What are you trying to do, Elliot?

ELLIOT: Well . . . say, we really want to do this. But the thing . . . the thing is, that kind of money is a little hard to come up with at this hour of the night. You understand? . . . No, we can't tomorrow . . . no, tomorrow I'm out of town. Say, would you consider, say, coming down a little? . . . Well, don't make a snap decision; ask your friend . . . but I have to tell you what we have here—we're emptying our wallets now—is, if we don't include our cab fare home, three hundred dollars. Yeah . . . well—well, I know. I know. I understand. I sure do. I sure do. . . . Well, let me tell you, you won't be sorry. . . . 440 East Ohio . . .

BOBBY: You can't bring 'em here!

ELLIOT: Apartment 22G.

BOBBY: Hey, man . . .

ELLIOT: Fifteen minutes? Sounds great to me, Fredericka. I'm
   sorry—Francine. (*Hangs up.*)

BOBBY: Call 'em back! Call 'em back! What the fuck are you doing?

ELLIOT: I don't ever want you to say I stop you.

BOBBY: Give me that goddamned card!

(ELLIOT *tears card into pieces, scatters pieces on floor.*)

   What the hell are you doing, man? You can't invite two
   tramps to my home! My *home!* My wife lives here, man! My
   wife and child! The women will be back in another hour! My
   boy's going to be home any minute!

ELLIOT: Then why did you show us the pictures, Bobby?

BOBBY: Shit, what's that got to do with it? He asked me! (*Indicates*
   PHIL.)

PHIL: I didn't ask you.

ELLIOT: You always do what Phil asks, Bobby?

PHIL: Bullshit he does!

ELLIOT: Is that what you're telling me? Why did you show us the
   business card?

BOBBY: What is this—an interrogation?

ELLIOT: Why did you turn on the cassette, Bobby?

BOBBY: Am I on trial? Here? In my own home? Are you putting me
   on trial? I turned it off in deference to you, buddy!

ELLIOT: I'm grateful. I'm grateful. Why did you put us through
   this, Bobby?

BOBBY: Put you through? Put you through what, motherfucker!

ELLIOT: You get a lot of pleasure out of it, don't you? Isn't that the
   case?

BOBBY: I try to do a favor. Is this what I get?

ELLIOT: Bobby, you are only trying to do one thing, and it's the same thing you've been trying to do since we were fourteen: you're trying to make your friends feel stupid, your best friends. Isn't that what's going on here? If I buy a new watch, you tell me where you could've gotten me a better deal. If I buy a stereo, you tell me what's wrong with it; the first thing, before I've had a chance to take an hour's pleasure, you tell me what a second-rate machine I've got. It doesn't matter what Consumers Union says: it's dated, it's warped, if I'd only talked to you. The deals you could have gotten me! And when I do go to you for advice? I don't get a deal, I get a smoke screen. I get words; I get so many ifs, ands, and buts, so much language, so much expertise, that I don't know whether I'm coming or going. But what I don't get, what I don't get is help. What I needed tonight was a little help. Larry, even Larry out there on the terrace, he tried to help.

LARRY: Come on, Elliot, you know Bobby.

ELLIOT: Phil tried to help. Vera, your wife, tried to help. What are you doing? These pictures and this . . . this cassette in your wife's house! What are you doing? What are you doing talking about family, the . . . the . . . the historic importance of family! Get in line, he says. If not this Joanna, some other Joanna. Maybe Fredericka? Maybe Francine? Am I going to march in line with Francine? Why do you have to do this to me tonight? All I wanted to do, all I wanted was to introduce my girl to my friends, my oldest friends. She was right all the time. She didn't want to know you.

PHIL: Come on, Elliot.

ELLIOT: I don't want to know you either.

BOBBY: You don't give a man a chance, do you, Elliot?

ELLIOT: I'll call the whores. I never intended for them to come.
  (*Picks up phone.*)

PHIL: You tore up the number!

ELLIOT: I remember it. (*Dials phone.*)

BOBBY: Who are you to judge? You've always been the judge.

PHIL (*to* ELLIOT): Well?

ELLIOT (*listens*): It's the answering machine for Bank of America.
  (*Hangs up, redials.*)

BOBBY: I've got a functioning marriage: I've got a fine wife and I've
  got a fine son. Who are you? What are you to tell me how to
  run my show?

ELLIOT: A show—that's all it is. You're not sincere about anything.
  (*Hangs up.*) Wrong number. I thought I remembered it.

(BOBBY *and* LARRY *scramble for pieces of the card.*)

  I thought I committed it to memory.

BOBBY: You'll pay, motherfucker!

ELLIOT: Oh, stop calling me "motherfucker"! It's too late to be
  black, Bobby. The only friends you have are white.

LARRY: Here it is.

BOBBY: Let me—

PHIL: 972-14—

(*Doorbell chimes. All look alarmed.*)

BOBBY: I'll kill you for this!

LARRY: I'll go.

BOBBY: This is my house. I will go.

LARRY: I'll go with you.

BOBBY: Shut the fuck up! Give me your money!

LARRY: Let's take a look. I want to see what I'm paying for.

PHIL: Larry's right. Maybe it's not the same girls.

BOBBY: I don't give a shit who it is, goddammit! I'm gonna pay the bitches off, and that's the end of it now! (*To* ELLIOT:) And I want you out of my house. And it ain't gonna be my money.

ELLIOT: It shouldn't be your money. (*Takes out wallet. To others:*) I'm sorry. (*Hands bills to* BOBBY.) It's only a hundred fifty.

(BOBBY *grabs the money and exits.*)

PHIL: Why do you say that, Elliot—you don't want to know us? We're your friends!

LARRY: Fuck him!

PHIL: You said it yourself: you don't have many friends. You know? You've got to keep the friends you have.

LARRY: Leave him alone. I painted his fucking apartment at cost!

PHIL: I've been on the wagon for three months. Sometimes you're really mean. I wouldn't do that to . . .

(*All suddenly stare at the study door as* JOANNA *enters. She stands alone, framed in the doorway.*)

JOANNA (*alarmed*): Elliot? . . . Where are the women?

CURTAIN

ACT 2

SCENE 1

The scene is Bobby's study, five minutes later. All eyes are on JOANNA, *sitting in Bobby's favorite chair. The others hover about, exhibiting small signs of nervousness.* PHIL *downs his Tab reflexively, jerkily.* LARRY *smirks at* JOANNA *across his bourbon glass.* ELLIOT *stands next to and a little behind her, warily, protectively.* BOBBY *is at the bar pouring a vodka and tonic. Throughout the scene, Bobby's accent ranges from Southern drawl to mid-Atlantic to clipped neo-British.*

BOBBY: Ice?

JOANNA: Piece of cake.

(BOBBY *mixes the drink amidst total silence. He serves* JOANNA.)

BOBBY: Girls should be back soon.

JOANNA: What was the movie?

(ELLIOT *and* PHIL *name movie simultaneously. In reaction, everyone takes a drink.*)

I didn't mean to blunder into a stag party.

ELLIOT (*quickly*): You missed a nice dinner, Joanna.

JOANNA: What did you have?

(*No one but* BOBBY *seems to remember.*)

LARRY: What—did—we—have?

BOBBY (*as if tasting it*): Couscous.

JOANNA: Forgive my ignorance. What exactly—?

BOBBY: Yeah, well, it's a North African dish. It's kind of a beef and chick-pea cereal. You understand?

JOANNA: Mm-hmm.

BOBBY: You kind of throw everything in the pantry into a pot: squash, zucchini, tomato paste, garlic. And when it achieves the consistency of motor oil, you pour the works on a what-have-you semolina-bran sort of concoction. Cholesterol count off the charts; guaranteed cardiac arrest.

JOANNA: Are you a cook, Bobby? You seem to know so much about it.

ELLIOT: Bobby taught Vera how to cook.

BOBBY: No way. She is nonpareil. My specialty is extraterrestrial condo-size omelettes.

(BOBBY *smiles at how well he's going over. Pause.* JOANNA *sits still, quietly drinking, as the men shift around.* JOANNA *turns to* LARRY.)

JOANNA: Larry, right?

LARRY: Yo.

JOANNA: Aren't you the one who drove your wife's car off the side of a mountain?

LARRY: It was only a cliff. It suited the purpose. It did the job. Anytime you want anyone's car driven off a cliff, I can give you tips. I'm your man.

JOANNA: My former husband, he didn't care so much about cars, but his true passion was his tape deck. Had I known you then I might have hired you to drop *that* off a cliff. I can't count the times I've thought of dropping it out a window. I guess I'm too much of a wimp.

PHIL: You're no wimp!

LARRY: Phil, will you never shut up.

(PHIL *looks away.* LARRY *grins at* ELLIOT.)

You want to know what you're letting yourself in for with this son of a bitch?

BOBBY: Larry's ready for bear, going to give you the real skinny. Oh, yeah.

LARRY: No. The lady has the right to know. He's a pseudointellectual, your Elliot. I'm telling it like it is here. When Bobby and Phil and me were reading Marvel comics at St. George . . .

(ELLIOT, BOBBY, *and* PHIL *ad-lib groans:* "Oh, no," "Lord save me.")

Give me a break here, guys, okay? Your boyfriend here was reading J.D. Salinger, who was a god to him—and who else was God to him at that point in time? Help me out, you guys.

PHIL: Ernest Hemingway.

BOBBY (*to* PHIL): Don't encourage him.

LARRY: That's right. That's right. And not only that. Not only that. When he read the papers—okay, he turned to sports first. I admit he was a little normal. But *after* sports, after the *comics*—

ELLIOT (*to* JOANNA): Forgive me.

LARRY: —the little bastard, the little show-off read the news columns!

BOBBY: Hey, man, we all read the news except you, you illiterate bastard!

LARRY: You read diddley! This bullshitter! Bobby is famous for his bullshit. Bobby won't even read the back of cornflakes boxes.

BOBBY: You must be tolerant. Larry is not comfortable with a woman outside the confines of a divorce court.

LARRY: Will ya listen to this bastard!

BOBBY: Larry will not date a lady without an attorney present.

LARRY (*grins*): The bastard's talking about my personal life! I'm not gonna let him get away with it. I'll tell you exactly what happened, Joanna. (*To* BOBBY:) I could talk about your personal life too, guy. (BOBBY *mock-shudders.*) So watch your tongue! (*To* JOANNA:) He's a great guy. Don't get him wrong.

ELLIOT: Say, Larry—

LARRY: Bobby would hide his light under a bushel, but he can't find one big enough. Huh? (*Turns to* ELLIOT *but turns back to* JOANNA *before* ELLIOT *can speak.*) What are you drinking?

(JOANNA *offers up her empty glass.* LARRY *crosses to bar.*)

JOANNA: Vodka and tonic.

LARRY (*at bar*): Out of ice. (*Heads for kitchen.*) Wait! I'll tell you the whole story. (*Exits.*)

JOANNA (*to* PHIL, *fast, before there can be a pause*): It's wonderful that you boys stayed fast friends. All these years. It's very rare.

PHIL: You're very different—I don't mean anything wrong—from Elliot's wife.

ELLIOT (*warning*): Phil . . .

PHIL (*shrugs*): No offense. (*Falls into silence.*)

JOANNA: Oh, poo. (*To* PHIL:) I'd like to hear.

(BOBBY *snickers.*)

PHIL: I mean, outside of looks. You look a little like her, but Marian was—she could say things—

JOANNA: That's interesting. I look like her?

ELLIOT: What is your problem, Phil?

PHIL: —could cut through you like a knife. Not to say she wasn't a smart girl. I'd have to say she was—well—way beyond me.

BOBBY (*cool*): Oh, that's hard.

PHIL: I mean, you're more at ease with us after five minutes than Marian after six years. She didn't approve of any of us. Bobby's got a point.

BOBBY (*confused, to* ELLIOT): What was my point?

PHIL: Although my wife—my then-wife—I'm separated— Ginger—and she's not as brilliant as Marian, but she didn't approve of these guys either. Including Elliot. I'm just saying—

BOBBY: Ginger may have been more brilliant than you think she was.

PHIL: Wives don't like their husbands' friends. Although Vera—

BOBBY: What they don't like is anyone who knows their old man better than they do.

PHIL: —Bobby's wife, she's not that way. Anyhow, if you know someone longer, it doesn't mean you know him necessarily—

BOBBY: Anyway, it's different, the way women know men.

PHIL: —better. The same man. You can take the same man and put him—

BOBBY: We are different with our wives than with our friends.

JOANNA (*laughs*): You're not better behaved. I can swear to that.

BOBBY: We show our weak side to our wives.

JOANNA: You put on less of a show. I'd agree with that.

BOBBY: We don't have to.

JOANNA: After you've got us. (*Laughs.*)

BOBBY: Riiight. After we gotcha, we want *you* to put on the show.

JOANNA: You don't want to do a damn thing. That's the truth of it.
   Oh, men, men. Lordy, lordy.

LARRY (*enters from kitchen carrying two drinks*): Elliot?

(ELLIOT *crosses to* LARRY, *standing by kitchen door. Others continue talking.*)

   The whores. I just remembered.

ELLIOT (*shocked*): Shit!

LARRY: Soon enough, old pal. What I'm saying—I'll head 'em off.
   In a couple of minutes I'll make an excuse, I'll excuse myself,
   and I'll go down to the lobby and I'll take care of it. They'll
   show up and I'll take care of it.

ELLIOT: What a jerk I am.

LARRY: You said it, not me.

ELLIOT: Thanks, Larry.

LARRY: No sweat. We'll settle up later.

ELLIOT: Thanks, Larry.

LARRY: I'll take care of it. Not another word. (*To* JOANNA:) Vodka
   and tonic. (*Brings her drink. Throughout the above, the following is intercut:*)

PHIL: Ginger was a lot like Marian, but they couldn't stand each other.

BOBBY: Maybe that's why.

PHIL: Ginger says anything that comes into her mind—it doesn't matter who's around—and she doesn't give a damn. Ya know? I mean I used to think she was a free spirit—am I boring you?—but after a while—I shouldn't complain—it's a little hard.

BOBBY: You're well out of it.

LARRY (*after serving Joanna's drink*): Who we talking about? I'll say she was hard, Ginger.

PHIL: Yeah, but she saw me through a lot.

LARRY: She drove you to drink.

PHIL: She had her good points.

LARRY (*to* JOANNA): Say, how did you two meet?

ELLIOT: You don't really want to know.

PHIL: *I* do.

JOANNA: Be nice, Elliot. You boys are going to love this! Where to begin? Ronnie, my eldest, going on seven, was running a fever and complaining of a stomachache, and the one thing I am decidedly not is a calm, cool, and collected mother. I know it's boring to hear me talk about my children, but— (*Smiles winningly.*) I am waiting for the doctor to return my call and—this is about seven in the evening and I have just gotten home and they never said a word at day care—they don't give two ticks, those girls. Well-meaning but ignorant, ignorant, ignorant, and I am not a racist. But I am in a state,

and the doctor has not called back, and my little girl is causing
a fuss the way they do when one is sick and receives all the
attention— (*To* LARRY:) I promise this gets better.

LARRY: No problem. (*Grins at her.*)

JOANNA: So of course, when the phone rings, I grab it on the
assumption it must be the doctor, but not at all: it's a young
man doing a survey, and I am as polite as I am able to be
under the circumstances, but I ask him courteously to get off
the phone, *please*, because I am with a sick child and I am
keeping the line open for the doctor. And the young man says,
"I appreciate that, but this will take only a moment of your
time. I'm going to list three leading beverages, and I wonder if
you could tell me which you'd be most likely to drink between
the hours of eight and eleven, eleven and two, two and five—"
So I asked to speak to his supervisor. I am livid. I am not often
livid, but the one thing that makes me livid is people who
know you are under duress but they have their agenda and, by
God, they are going to stick to it. So I ask—I demand—the
name of his superior, and I won't bore you with how long *that*
took or what he said, the little weasel, or what I said in reply.
But shameful as it is to say, in the time spent on that, the
doctor might have been calling and calling and calling. I'd
never know. But I have lost interest in my ailing calf. I want
this man's job! And when I finally am put in contact with his
superior, why, it's Elliot! And I explain to him as he comes on
the phone that I can't talk to him now, but if I could have his
name and telephone number, he has a young man in his
employ that I would like him to fire. And he paused only a
brief second and said, "I'd be pleased to fire anyone you want
me to; I will be waiting for your call, Mrs. Ross." Now wasn't
that the most charming thing to say?

PHIL: Did he fire him?

JOANNA: He did not. He lied. This man, your friend, lied to me. Can you believe he would do that to me?

LARRY: Can I get you another drink, Joanna?

JOANNA: I believe the man is trying to get me drunk. (*Reaches over and touches Elliot's arm affectionately.*) I didn't know him the way I know him now. He's too kind to fire anybody.

ELLIOT: I fire people.

JOANNA: Poo you have!

LARRY: Did they know they were fired after you fired them?

ELLIOT: I don't throw them bodily out of the office.

LARRY: You tell them you think they'd be happier elsewhere.

ELLIOT: I tell them—

LARRY (*interrupts*): "This hurts me more than it hurts you."

JOANNA: Be still now, Larry. (*Puts a hand out, nearly touching him. LARRY grins.*)

ELLIOT: —just that it's not working out, that I'm sorry it's not working out, and if they want to talk about it I'd be happy to do that, but if they prefer not, that's fine too.

LARRY: You're too goddamn nice! (ELLIOT *shrugs.*) Somebody you fire, it probably takes a month before he knows you've fired him. When I fire an employee it's because they're incompetent, and incompetence puts me in a rage.

JOANNA: You too? Me too!

LARRY: In a rage!

JOANNA: Especially my own. I can't stand my own.

BOBBY: You can't stand incompetence? You are living in the wrong age.

JOANNA: It does seem to be everywhere, doesn't it?

BOBBY: I am competent. I am an extremely competent man. But at the magazine I dare not show it.

JOANNA: Where do you work, Bobby? I should know this.

ELLIOT and BOBBY (*together*): *Playboy.*

JOANNA: *Playboy.*

LARRY: Now we're talking incompetence.

BOBBY: If you expose your competence—overly expose your competence—to colleagues who are less competent than they perceive you to be, they will react badly. They will react in a hostile manner. You understand what I am saying?

JOANNA: It's everywhere, kind of, isn't it?

BOBBY: It's a threat.

JOANNA: Competence is a threat.

BOBBY: Precisely.

JOANNA: Because you overshadow them. I mean—

BOBBY: If you are the best in a situation where they know it and you know it but they are afraid of it, they reject it. So be it. Understand?

LARRY: Right. Fuck it! My man, Bobby.

PHIL: Come on—watch your language, Larry. (*To* JOANNA:) I'm sorry.

JOANNA (*to* PHIL): I like to hear men curse. Although the language my children already use!

LARRY: It's women cursing that gets me.

BOBBY: Larry's old lady, she could turn the air purple.

PHIL: That's one good thing about Ginger—

LARRY (*grins at* ELLIOT): Marian could say "fuck" more naturally than Elliot. Elliot's a bit of a prude. But I guess you know that. Marian Fogarty could dish it out with the best of them.

PHIL: And then switch to the most highfalutin—

BOBBY: Jesus, I almost forgot that!

LARRY: This movie is Felliniesque, and that movie is Bergmanesque. She could have been a critic.

(*All the men but* ELLIOT *laugh.* ELLIOT *looks anxiously at* JOANNA.)

JOANNA: I love profanity. It's so—I think it can be poetic the way men use it. I'm not at ease when it's used by women as much. Are you? But did you see this play that was in Chicago a couple of years ago? These real estate salesmen? Glen—Glen something? Impossible title! My, the way they jawed at each other. I'm in real estate and that's not *quite* the way these people talk. But it's poetic license.

LARRY: I see movies—mainly videotapes. Believe it, nothing Felliniesque. There's no theater worth seeing in Chicago.

BOBBY: Look who's the authority. (*Shakes his head sagely.*)

JOANNA: Are you a theater buff, Bobby? Elliot won't ever take me.

ELLIOT: You never told me you wanted to go.

BOBBY: You see *Fences*?

JOANNA: I did indeed. When it played here. Remarkable, if you want my opinion. Remarkable.

ELLIOT: Of course I'll take you to the theater.

BOBBY: That was my story.

JOANNA: No.

BOBBY: My story. My father was that father. I'm different from the son, but that was my father. Except he wasn't a good ball-player. But pride. Fucked-up, stupid, jive-assed pride. Male profanity.

JOANNA: Just lovely.

BOBBY: My father died at forty-two, which is my next birthday. From the time I was fourteen, I was bigger and stronger and better coordinated than my father. Not as heavy, though. No way. My father was the original butterball. Mr. Five-by-Five. Loved to throw that ball. Did he ever! And moved pretty good for a man his girth. He had these dainty little feet, god-damnedest feet! My mother's feet were bigger. Toes the size of cucumbers. An ox, my mother. But my father, you under-stand, he had a good arm on him. And he could rifle a throw in from right field, nail a man turning third, never make it home. I saw him do it more than once. But he couldn't get around on a fastball. This particular Sunday—did I say I'm fourteen?—I struck him out twice. Fathers-and-sons game. Hyde Park, you understand, and I was a big kid. Oh, was I! On my mother's side they're all six feet and over. But I worshipped the man. Like in *Fences*. Father and son. Like in *Bambi*. Where the stags fight. So now I struck out Bambi's father, and he has trouble meeting my eye. I'm fourteen years old and I don't weigh a hundred and thirty, and two strikeouts later I'm king of the stags. My father abdicates. Everybody struck the old fool out! It was never the same.

JOANNA: And he died shortly thereafter.

BOBBY (*after a pause*): Nooo. (*Pause.*) It would have made a better story, wouldn't it? (*Smiles at* JOANNA.) Eight years later. I'm sorry. He died eight years later. Another? (*Takes her glass.*)

JOANNA: You're in AA, Phil?

LARRY (*before* PHIL *can answer*): I was gonna tell you about my wife. These guys thought they knew her. (*Shakes his head.*) I gotta tell you: twenty-one days PMS. (*Throughout his speech,* LARRY *cannot look at* JOANNA.) "What's the matter with your hair, Larry?" "You smell funny." I mean, what's the matter with my hair? Nothing's the matter with my hair. It's my hair, all right?! The hair she was sleeping with, *stroking*. Every night for three years. That's my hair. The same fucking hair. You better believe it, it's hilarious. But the minuses are the minuses, and when the pluses outweigh the minuses, "What's the matter with your hair?" is a joke; and when the minuses outweigh the pluses, it's a good reason to drive the bitch's car off a cliff.

(*An embarrassed silence.*)

ELLIOT: Larry, didn't you have somewhere to go?

LARRY (*looks at his watch, swills down his drink*): Now I'll tell you about my father. I had a father too. (*Addresses* JOANNA:) My father didn't talk. Maybe he talked to my sisters. They got along fine. But he couldn't talk to me. Son of a bitch. A tenant in the house, that's what he was. He hung around weekends. He paid my mother rent. He was good with small talk, that he could do. Courteous. Genial. He could tell he knew me from somewhere; he just couldn't fit my face with a name. He called me by my sisters' names. I grew up believing—hoping—he wasn't my real father. Maybe I was adopted, it was my only hope. A mistake in the hospital.

PHIL: Your father was a great guy—what are you talking about?

(LARRY *shrugs, goes to pour himself a drink*.)

ELLIOT: Now I guess we have to hear about your father, Phil. Larry, it's getting late.

(LARRY *returns with a drink, doesn't answer.*)

Didn't you have somewhere to go?

LARRY (*looks at his watch*): Couple of minutes. This is fun. I like your girl, El. I could never talk to my wife.

(*He moves close to* JOANNA. JOANNA *smoothly turns to* PHIL.)

JOANNA: I admire you for not drinking, Phil. I wish I could give it up.

PHIL: You have to do it one day at a time.

JOANNA: I can't do anything one day at a time.

PHIL: You don't need it. Nobody needs it.

LARRY: I need it.

BOBBY (*nods*): Heaven help us.

PHIL: It's an addiction.

ELLIOT: Joanna is not an alcoholic. This is getting depressing.

PHIL: It's drinking that depresses you, Elliot.

ELLIOT: The talking, Phil, the talking about drinking depresses me.

JOANNA (*to* ELLIOT): Don't let it get to you.

PHIL: I'm not being holier than thou.

ELLIOT: Give it a rest, all right?

PHIL: I'm not, Elliot. Say I'm not.

ELLIOT: Isn't it good enough that you've stopped? Joanna doesn't have a drinking problem.

PHIL: You don't?

JOANNA: I could have.

PHIL: I thought you had a drinking problem.

JOANNA: I have what you might call a small, ungifted drinking problem. I drink. I do drink.

PHIL: Well, there you are. (*To* ELLIOT:) Elliot?

JOANNA: Well, it's true I don't—too much. That's certainly true. I have very little capacity.

PHIL: So you stopped.

JOANNA: But I wish I didn't have to. I hate women drunks—and that, I believe, is what stops me. Women drunks are unattractive. And you men, you men can get away with it.

BOBBY: The lady has drinking envy.

JOANNA: That's very clever of you, Bobby.

BOBBY: That's what you've got, drinking envy.

JOANNA: I would like to be able to get away with drinking like a man.

PHIL: No, you wouldn't. And I'm not being holier than thou when I say that. (*To* ELLIOT:) I'm not, Elliot. You know me.

JOANNA: Oh, poo, Elliot. Phil is not being holier than thou.

PHIL: You don't know me, but that's not the kind of person I am.

JOANNA: I'd just bet on it.

ELLIOT: I didn't say you were being holier than thou—

LARRY: Yes, you did.

ELLIOT: What I meant—

LARRY (*with sarcasm*): Oh, now he's going to tell us what he meant! Deep, the man's deep.

ELLIOT: You talk too damn much about not drinking.

PHIL: I didn't bring it up.

ELLIOT: Whoever brings it up, you do talk about it, Phil. Come on—you know it and Larry knows it and Bobby knows it.

BOBBY: Don't tell me what I know, man! I don't know it.

ELLIOT (*glares at him*): Good. I don't know it either.

JOANNA (*to* ELLIOT): Now you be nice.

LARRY: None of us knows it. (*Finishes drink.*)

JOANNA (*to* ELLIOT): Don't let it get to you.

LARRY: I take it one day at a time. (*Pours himself another drink.*)

BOBBY: Hear, hear.

JOANNA: Scott Fitzgerald said, "First, you take a drink. Then the drink takes a drink. Then the drink takes you."

PHIL: That's right. That's true. Fitzgerald said that?

JOANNA: I believe so.

PHIL: That's very good, you know? "First, you take a drink. Then the drink takes a drink. Then the drink takes you." That's what happens, you know? Exactly what happens. (*Nods vigorously.*) That's exactly what happens.

JOANNA: It must take great strength of character. (*Pause.*) I am so weak-willed. (*Pause.*) Elliot knows how weak-willed I am.

ELLIOT: Goddammit! You're not weak-willed, Joanna, you're about the strongest woman I know!

JOANNA: Listen to the man rave. I am so weak-willed I cannot resist a sale.

(*Pause.*)

BOBBY (*beams paternally at* JOANNA): Capitalism, my dear. We live in a society that forbids us to resist a sale. We are so programmed. The American disease.

ELLIOT: I can't believe this!

JOANNA: Oh, I bet you can resist anything you put your mind to, Bobby.

BOBBY: I am not of this system. I'm of another system. I dip into this system and use it however it suits me. I've trained myself to do just that. You understand what I'm saying?

ELLIOT: Larry, are you going downstairs or not? You said you were going.

LARRY: What's the hurry?

(ELLIOT *crosses to bar and pours a stiff drink. He holds it out to* PHIL.)

ELLIOT: Do us all a favor, Phil. You used to be a great guy. Nobody can stand you anymore.

(*All freeze*, ELLIOT *with a drink held out to* PHIL, *who looks stunned. Finally* LARRY *crosses to* ELLIOT, *takes the drink, and downs it.*)

LARRY (*to* JOANNA): Nice meeting you. You spend your lifetime looking for a woman. There comes a time— I'm getting ready. (*He crosses to the door.*) I got a fourteen-day advance-record cable-ready VCR. I got games racked up on tape: the whole Laker-Celtic series, Super Bowl XI, every Muhammed Ali fight going back to Liston, Hagler-Leonard, Leonard-Duran. I got *Pal Joey, Magnum Force, The Good, the Bad and the Ugly.* I got more than seven hundred hours on tape. The times I spend with a woman—what's it come to, the times awake? Five, six hours a night, and weekends. Half of it hassle. The VCR is better. A chicken-and-pasta takeout. I open a brew, I rack up the VCR. No regrets, no recriminations, no consequences. My companion.

BLACKOUT

SCENE 2

Time: later that night, four a.m. Dark stage. The telephone rings five times with increasing loudness. Lights up, stage right, Elliot's living room.

ELLIOT *is sprawled in a beat-up armchair. That, plus a side table with a telephone and a floor lamp, makes up the scenery. An open* Chicago Tribune *and* Time *magazine lie crumpled at his feet. His jacket, tie, and shoes are off. A half-empty bottle of Scotch sits on the side table next to a watery ice tray. A Scotch glass rests on the arm of the chair.* ELLIOT *has been lying, passed out, in the chair for about an hour. He stares angrily at the phone, deciding whether to answer, and when he does, his voice is hoarse with sleep and booze.*

ELLIOT: I don't think there's anything left for us to say.

(*Lights up, stage left, Joanna's kitchen.* JOANNA *sits on a high stool next to a white wall phone. She wears a nightgown and robe, and is barefoot. A pot of coffee sits on a table nearby. She holds a mug in her hand, which she sips at. She will refill the mug throughout the scene until the pot is empty.*)

JOANNA: Surely we can talk. We're adults. I don't want to leave it like this.

(ELLIOT *starts to reply, says nothing. Long pause.*)
        Can you come over? (*Pause.*) Are you there?

ELLIOT: No.

JOANNA: No, you're not there?

ELLIOT: No, I can't come over.

JOANNA: I think what you're doing is very hurtful to both of us, Elliot.

ELLIOT: Okay. (*Pause.*) You come over here.

JOANNA: I've got the children. How can I?

ELLIOT (*icy*): I'd say you've got a problem.

JOANNA: I've never heard you so mean.

ELLIOT: If that's what you called for, to call me names, if that's it—

JOANNA: Please—

ELLIOT: I'm going to hang up this phone.

JOANNA: Elliot, what is happening here? We've got to talk!

ELLIOT: Why?

JOANNA: Don't you think so?

ELLIOT: Not really.

JOANNA: What have I missed? Did I do something? I don't know what you think I did, Elliot.

ELLIOT: I don't think (*long pause*) what happened tonight can be explained away, Joanna—

JOANNA: Very little happened tonight, as far as I can tell. I met your friends. I liked them. (*Pause.*) Is there nothing you want to say to me? (*Pause.*) Elliot?

ELLIOT: You're the one who called.

(A *long pause.* JOANNA *waits for more.* ELLIOT *says nothing. He puts down the phone, exits, reenters with a full ice tray, puts ice in his glass, and pours a Scotch. He sips it and makes a sour face. He glares at the phone and picks it up. Throughout the above,* JOANNA *doesn't move except for occasional sips of coffee. She is listening hard.*)

The worst part . . . what I cannot get over . . . what I cannot forgive is Phil.

JOANNA: I liked Phil. I really don't understand what you are trying to do here.

ELLIOT: You patronized Phil. Phil is an unstable guy, Joanna, who has never been very strong. But he is decent and he is sweet, and he would never dream of speaking a word he doesn't mean . . . which is why he has trouble getting words out, because unlike you, he wants to be certain he means them.

(*Goes into a coughing fit.*)

You came onto Phil as if you were an alcoholic—

JOANNA: Are you all right?

(*No response.*)

I did no such thing.

ELLIOT: As a drunk, then.

JOANNA: I *do* drink.

ELLIOT: You don't drink, Joanna. Not the way Phil means it. But you made it sound as if you were colleagues in AA, peer drunks, you and Phil. "A small, ungifted drinking problem." My God! "I wish I could get drunk like you big bad men do, but women drunks are so unattractive." Jesus Christ!

JOANNA: He liked me!

ELLIOT: They *all* liked you. They fell for you like a ton of bricks. Even Larry, who hates women. "Incompetence puts me in a rage," he says, talking about—about how I can't fire people, talking about what a wimp I am, Joanna! I don't put up with incompetent employees! Why do you put me in a position where I have to defend myself? Not with my friends! But do

you take my side? Is there a shred of loyalty? You see the
opening to—to get on Larry's side and you dive right in. You
plough right in. "How true. How true. Incompetence puts me
in a rage too." For Christ's sake! For Christ's sake!

JOANNA: You must be out of your mind.

ELLIOT: You see? I could have predicted this. You wanted me to
talk. I'm talking. But you don't want to hear it, so I'm out of
my mind. What's the use?

JOANNA: Don't get upset.

ELLIOT: *Don't say that!*

(*Pause.*)

JOANNA: All the way home in the taxi, not a single word. Not a
sentence. Certainly none of this. Rather, the abuse of your
moroseness. Silence. Your deep, penetrating, opaque, manly
gloom. I pay off the sitter and you follow her out the door.
Within seconds after she's gone, you are gone. No argument.
No explanation. I have the right to expect a sentence or two. I
expect—however stumbling, stammering, what have you—I
expect *reasons!*

ELLIOT (*furious*): I do not stammer, Joanna. You are confusing me
with other men in your life. Other men who you no doubt
seduced the way you seduced my friends tonight. (*Mock
Southern syrupy.*) "My former husband, Jo Bob, now he
didn't care beans about cars—y'heah? His truly great passion
was his tape deck. I would have gladly hired you to drop his
tape deck off a cliff."

(JOANNA *hangs up.*)

Bitch!

(*He quickly dials the phone.* JOANNA *picks up before the first ring is complete.*)

I'll tell you something about Ginger—Phil's wife, Ginger. Maybe you need a little context here, although God knows I don't know if anything will help.

JOANNA: I will listen. Please try to stay calm.

ELLIOT: Try not to say you're listening when you're talking and not listening. Try to be honest if you can be honest. I don't know if—

JOANNA: I'm about to hang up again.

ELLIOT: It has always driven me crazy, these phrases of yours—

JOANNA: Now it comes out.

ELLIOT: These phrases: "don't let it get to you," "don't get upset." And worst of all . . . worst of all when you said "piece of cake" tonight not three minutes after you were in the room with my friends. You want to know something? Something truly riotous? I wanted to die at that moment. I literally cringed. Literally cringed. I felt stripped naked. I knew at that moment, with that first "piece of cake," I knew that this was going to be a disaster.

JOANNA: No one but you thinks it was a disaster. No one but you had a bad time.

ELLIOT: A bad time? I had one of the classic bad times of the century! I had not one bad time but two very different interweaving bad times. First, seeing my friends make asses of themselves over you—they couldn't help themselves—

JOANNA: It was an awkward situation, I was trying to help. *You* didn't help.

ELLIOT: —and second . . . second, seeing how you really are with
men. Alone I never saw it. Too close. Too close. But it was like
a laboratory, seeing you work, seeing you teasing and manip-
ulating like mice, rodents, lab animals. These poor—Ginger,
. . . Before you hang up again—and don't think I'm calling
you back—you hang up this time, that's it for life, sister.
Believe it! Ginger was Larry's girl. Then she was Bobby's.
They used to pass girls around, the two of them. A big joke.
And Phil, Phil fell in love with every girl they discarded. Just
about. Phil believes all women come from another and better
planet, and the ones who slept with Larry and Bobby attain
the status—I don't know—something like First Lady. Jackie
Onassis. God, the way Phil looked at you. The way he looked
at you. Okay. Are you there?

JOANNA: I suppose I am.

ELLIOT: She was never very steady. I liked her all right. I nearly took
her out. Ginger, I mean. After Bobby, before Larry. I won't go
out with a girl after Larry's through with her. Larry and I have
this thing— Where was I? You there? Anyhow, Ginger is a
big, strapping girl, and Phil, who's easygoing enough—you
can see that—is always after her . . . *was* always after her to
keep her weight in line, or at least stay in shape, exercise, or
whatever the hell idea he had in mind for her to do. Iso-
metrics. Yoga. Whatever. And he's really on her case. For
Phil, that is, who really can't get on anyone's case. But to the
extent that he's able to be forceful— Anyhow, she does it,
signs up for a yoga class. And the day his mother goes to the
hospital with cancer, Phil calls up Ginger—they don't even
know what it is at the time, but an ambulance took her so you
can't say Joanna didn't know it was important—I mean Ginger. Ginger knew it was important but she said, "I have to go
to my yoga class." And Phil is on the phone to her, this whole
thing happens on the telephone. He says, "But my mother's in

the hospital." And Ginger says, "You're the one who wanted me to get in shape, and now I signed up and you don't want me to go. Make up your mind, Phil." (*Pause.*) Make up your mind, Phil. Make up your mind, Phil. And wouldn't you know it? He ended up convinced it was his fault.

JOANNA: I don't know why it is you're telling this story.

ELLIOT: Just to show you. That's the kind of guy he is. That's all. That's what he is, and you shouldn't have— I'm not suggesting that Ginger made him an alcoholic. He comes from a family of heavy drinkers. But . . . (*Trails off.*)

JOANNA: I wasn't the one who offered him a drink.

(ELLIOT *gasps.*)

I wasn't the one who tried to force—actually challenge—my alcoholic friend to take a drink, Elliot. That wasn't me.

ELLIOT: It was you.

JOANNA: No, it was you.

ELLIOT: It was everything you did that led up to it.

JOANNA: It wasn't me.

ELLIOT: You can't take it out of context.

JOANNA: It wasn't me.

ELLIOT: You're trying to do what Ginger did. There's a context . . .

JOANNA: Maybe there was a context for Ginger refusing to go to the hospital—

ELLIOT: What, a yoga class?! What kind of context is that? Don't defend her just because you did something tonight—

JOANNA: Maybe there was something between Ginger and Phil's mother. Or between themselves. Don't try to judge what married people do to each other, Elliot. The reasons are never clear. It's never clear what goes on between two people. They don't even have to be married. Look at us. What is our context? I don't know. Do you know? I don't know why I'm on one end of the phone and you're on the other end having a farewell fight with me when we both expected to be here at this hour together in bed.

ELLIOT: I never felt right about that.

JOANNA: This is not my idea.

ELLIOT: You insist on misunderstanding everything I say. What's the point? Our being in bed together under the same roof as your kids. That doesn't bother you?

JOANNA: Elliot, I don't intend to sit here passively—

ELLIOT: It doesn't even bother you, the morality of it? They hear everything that goes on.

JOANNA: No, they don't, and I'll tell you why: they are children. They are asleep. They sleep through garbage trucks and warbling ambulances and low-flying jets.

ELLIOT: It's wrong, goddammit!

JOANNA: What am I supposed to do—farm them out? I have nowhere to send them.

ELLIOT: Your parents.

JOANNA: You want me to send my babies away to my parents so that you can fuck me with a clear conscience? Is that what this argument is really about?

ELLIOT: I don't believe this! It's about—I'll tell you what it's about. Your cavalier screw-it-all attitude that services your needs moment by moment—and you have all the charm in the world to get away with it—but you don't take into account the effect this has on others.

JOANNA: You are uncomfortable with sex, Elliot.

(*He hangs up and sits there. She finishes her coffee, pulls a bottle of gin from under the counter and pours a healthy shot, takes a snort, and dials the phone.* ELLIOT *picks up.*)

You are uncomfortable with sex, Elliot. You know it and I know it. Though we have never talked about it.

ELLIOT: I'm uncomfortable with hypocrisy, not sex. I don't like living in the kind of world where in order to take my pleasure— Don't tell me they don't sense something.

JOANNA: That is my business, not yours. They like you, Elliot. They admire you. They talk about you. They're always asking me questions about you.

ELLIOT: When my sister brought boys home, I heard everything.

JOANNA: They are not being injured. I would not allow it.

ELLIOT: If you feel more comfortable thinking that—

JOANNA: You haven't allowed me to feel comfortable since we met. Truly comfortable. You worry about everything and I worry about you worrying.

ELLIOT: The hell you do!

JOANNA: Just because I don't make a show of it. You put on enough show. All that heartfelt concern of yours. All that sensitivity. Don't talk to me about thoughtfulness. You vacuum up all the thoughtfulness in the room. You leave nothing for others. You're anticipating, always anticipating, questioning, preplanning. You don't have a spontaneous bone in that tight-, tight-, tightassed, disapproving, harsh, judgmental body.

(*Pause.*)

ELLIOT: I am judgmental. I know that.

JOANNA: All right then. So am I.

ELLIOT: No, you're not.

JOANNA: No one on God's green earth is as judgmental as you are. But believe me, that notwithstanding, I *am* judgmental, Elliot. I have passed a thousand judgments on you.

(*Pause.*)

ELLIOT: You don't think it's wrong what we're doing to your children?

JOANNA: Everything is wrong, Elliot. You can't be with children without being wrong. You can't be with people without making one bonehead mistake after another. So you pick up. That's all life is: picking up after. Picking up.

ELLIOT: I don't agree with that.

JOANNA: You don't have children. You don't make mistakes. You don't get tied up in knots with other people.

ELLIOT: I got tied up with you.

JOANNA: And now you've found a way of getting untied.

ELLIOT: That's not what's happening.

JOANNA: No? Then what is? Tell me.

(*Pause.*)

ELLIOT: I'm not sure anymore. I was sure before. I'm not so sure.

(*Pause.*) Joanna, I don't really think I can be in the wrong about this. (*Pause.*)

JOANNA: I'm still here.

ELLIOT: What did you mean by that?

JOANNA: Only that I'm listening.

ELLIOT: Don't do that. I meant—you know what I meant. That you have passed judgment on me a thousand times.

JOANNA: I have passed judgment. Unlike you, I have not passed sentence.

ELLIOT: I see. You've been magnanimous with me. I've been small-minded, but you're—Joanna's magnamanamous.

JOANNA (*cool*): Magnanimous.

ELLIOT (*heatedly*): I know the word. What makes you so goddamn superior! Where do you get off! How dare you condescend to me!

JOANNA: I never condescend to you.

ELLIOT: Yes, you do.

JOANNA: I didn't condescend to you tonight—

ELLIOT: To the others. I'm not talking about me tonight. Other times—

JOANNA: I condescended to you.

ELLIOT: You know it!

JOANNA: When have I done that, Elliot?

ELLIOT: Right this minute. Right this minute! Listen, if you could hear the sound of your own voice.

JOANNA: I am defending myself with this voice. You are attacking me, and I am defending myself. But when I am not defending myself, tell me one time, one single time, that I have condescended to you—

ELLIOT: You want names and dates?

JOANNA: Because it is not true. I have respected you.

ELLIOT: Passed judgment! You said it yourself.

JOANNA: So do you!

ELLIOT: Not on you.

JOANNA: But you can't stand it when I say "piece of cake."

ELLIOT: Big deal.

JOANNA: It makes you feel stripped naked.

ELLIOT: Tonight. Only tonight. Again, you're screwing around with context.

JOANNA: Other times it doesn't bother you.

ELLIOT: It always bothers me. But there's a difference between bothering me and stripping me naked.

JOANNA: Why does it bother you?

ELLIOT: Because—because— You're a smart girl. Do I really have to explain?

JOANNA: I'm afraid that you really do.

ELLIOT: Because it's thoughtless.

JOANNA: Mean old me.

ELLIOT: It's—it's automatic pilot. When you say it to me—or those other things, those other things you say—it's not addressed to me, Elliot; it's addressed to anonymous.

JOANNA: I see. I make you feel anonymous.

ELLIOT: At those times, yes.

JOANNA: But not at other times.

ELLIOT: At other times . . . at other times . . . (*Breaks into sobs.*) No one ever made me feel the way you do. (*Struggles for control.*)

JOANNA (*losing control*): Elliot . . .

ELLIOT: I'm all right . . . Joanna.

JOANNA: Shall I tell you how I feel? I feel as if I've been mugged.

ELLIOT: I never cared for anyone the way I care for you, and you mind it. You think I'm a fussbudget. You see, we get it all wrong with each other.

JOANNA: I didn't say that.

ELLIOT: But that's the way it comes out. I think I'm doing one thing. I think I'm being considerate, and you don't see it as considerate. You see it as a vacuum cleaner.

JOANNA: No . . .

ELLIOT: I vacuum-clean up all the emotions. And when you say it I can see that, yes, that's what I do. She's right. That's exactly what I do. But that's not— I thought, I thought I was doing something else. When you think you're doing something right, and it's wrong— When you think—when you set out to deliberately please someone, and the very act is a turn-off—

JOANNA: It's not that drastic.

ELLIOT: How can that gap be bridged? There's a gap. A gap, Joanna. And I—what I do—I guess—I try to bridge it, and I make it wider. I only wanted you to like me. It was important for me to have you care for me.

JOANNA: Don't you know that I do?

ELLIOT: I wanted to be special in your life, but everything I did—

JOANNA: It doesn't matter.

ELLIOT: It's the only thing that does matter. Whether people narrow the gap or widen it—isn't that what decides whether they should be together?

JOANNA: I don't think there are rules for this sort of thing, Elliot.

ELLIOT: There have to be.

JOANNA: Well then, the rules don't work.

ELLIOT: There has to be something. Or else how do we know?

JOANNA: I don't know. Talking can help. We've never discussed these things before.

ELLIOT: Talking can't help.

JOANNA: Maybe it can help.

ELLIOT: I'm a polltaker, Joanna. I talk to people all the time. None of it is real. And you're in real estate.

JOANNA: You thought I was doing that to your friends tonight. Selling them. Setting them up.

ELLIOT: Setting them up.

JOANNA: That's what made you so upset.

ELLIOT (*heatedly*): *Not upset!*

JOANNA (*quickly*): Mad. Mad.

ELLIOT: I know you didn't like them.

JOANNA: I did like them.

ELLIOT: That's more talk. Listen, I've got to tell you I wouldn't like them either if I hadn't grown up with them. But what was I supposed to do when I see you with them—the way you were with them—so winning, so charming, so incredibly interested in what they're saying, as if whoever it is you're talking to, he's the only person who exists in the world. Larger than life, Joanna. That's the way you are with me. And I could see it was—there's no other way of saying it—a game to you. What was I supposed to think?

JOANNA: You think I tricked you?

ELLIOT: I think— What am I supposed to think?

JOANNA: That I don't mean a word I say.

ELLIOT: . . . You tricked me. I thought—this is what I thought—that you felt—a certain way about me—this is humiliating—and it turns out to be—technique. You turn it on—

JOANNA: I'm a phony.

ELLIOT: Are you?

JOANNA: If you have to ask. . . . Maybe it is too wide a gap. I can't ask you some of the things you ask me. If you have to ask what a relationship costs, young man, you can't afford one. I'm not the way you are, Elliot. I assume certain things. I don't relentlessly examine my assumptions. I assume if we're together for six weeks, there's a good reason for that. No? I do make judgments, granted. So do you. But that doesn't turn a good reason into a bad reason. I don't know. Or does it?

ELLIOT: I don't know.

JOANNA: Well, I don't know either. So talking doesn't help. We've pretty well dispensed with that illusion. What helps, Elliot?

(*Silence.*)

Anything? Anything at all?

(*Silence.*)

I don't know what there is left to do. We do understand things
differently. We do miss connections. I'm sure that's true. You
do with me all the time. I was arrogant enough to think I
didn't with you. You see, I am probably most of everything
bad you think of me. But my effect is not calculated. What
you call a "technique." It's not a technique. I have four
brothers whom I never mentioned and with whom I'm not in
contact. I loved them passionately as a child. I have no
addresses for them and I worry, what if I die, how will they
know? And that's my only reason for resuming contact: so that
they will be informed when I die. I have arranged a life that
belongs to no one. I am not home, Elliot. You asked me about
my children and our having sex in the next room. I think they
don't hear. I'm sure they don't hear. But until you asked, the
question never occurred to me. I live in this state—I don't
know how to describe it, guilt is a step up from where I am
now—a state of moral absenteeism. I want no encumbrances.
I'm on loan to my children, but only till they're old enough
for me to run away from. I have two close friends whom you
will never meet, Fay and Walter. They adore me and I adore
them, and we are intimates and they know nothing about me.
I chose to like you because I thought—this is cruel—I thought
you were safe.

ELLIOT: I'm safe all right.

JOANNA: I thought I could keep you in bounds. I used to think it was
a love of freedom that motivated my bad judgments.

ELLIOT: Am I a bad judgment?

JOANNA: You are right to be angry. I am better with your friends than I am with you. I am at my most devastating with strangers. It used to vex and astonish me how much better my mother was with my friends than with her own children. No, Elliot, my bad judgment was that I could contain you.

ELLIOT: Joanna . . .

JOANNA: I didn't dislike your friends. I liked them better than my friends. Phil and Bobby, not Larry. They remind me of my brothers, and they look up to you so.

ELLIOT: That's crazy.

JOANNA: Of course, to you. It made me proud.

ELLIOT: What I did to Phil is unforgivable.

JOANNA: He understands.

ELLIOT: Unforgivable. It was the worst single thing I have ever done in my life. How can he understand?

JOANNA: You'll call him.

ELLIOT: How can I call him? How can I speak to any of them ever again?

JOANNA: You were under great stress . . .

ELLIOT: That's no excuse. There is no excuse. It's a betrayal of every principle—

JOANNA: You can't always be in control—

ELLIOT: Is that what it amounts to? And when I'm not in control I'm a worse asshole than the rest of them?

JOANNA: You will call him, Elliot, and you will apologize. And he will be grateful for your call. He adores you, that man.

ELLIOT: You're a much better person than I am.

JOANNA: Lordy—

ELLIOT: I'm such a disappointment.

JOANNA: Not to me!

ELLIOT: Okay, to myself. I'm not like you. I'm a failure.

JOANNA: No, you're not!

ELLIOT: I don't even care anymore. Much more was expected of me.

JOANNA: My mother still talks about how it's not too late for me to go to law school. All my friends think I'm throwing my life away.

ELLIOT: You never told me that.

JOANNA: Uh-huh.

ELLIOT: I've done better than my father, as a matter of fact. How come we've never had this conversation before?

JOANNA: We have.

ELLIOT: Have we? When I go home, my father has trouble looking at me. My voice cracks when I go home.

JOANNA: Do it for me.

ELLIOT: What?

JOANNA: Crack your voice like when you're at your father's.

ELLIOT: I can't. (*Pause.*) Hi, Mom. Hi (*voice cracks*), Dad.

(JOANNA *screams with laughter.* ELLIOT *starts to laugh.*)

I'm sorry, Joanna—I'm so sorry. I'm so sorry.

JOANNA: Stop that!

ELLIOT: I'm a lousy lover.

JOANNA: I didn't say that. I don't think that.

ELLIOT: I've never—I don't understand sex. It scares me, after all these years. It doesn't scare you.

JOANNA: I'm scared for you. So much is going on inside that head of yours.

ELLIOT: When we're in bed.

JOANNA: Boom-biddy-boom-biddy-boom, the drums and the horns and—I can't help but say it—

ELLIOT: What?

JOANNA: The bugle call of retreat.

ELLIOT: You know so much more than I thought you knew. The pleasure in my life comes from committing acts I'm morally opposed to. I'm a prude. Everything that makes me happy is in absolute defiance of my own standards.

JOANNA: You have strong values.

ELLIOT: I don't have values, I have sentiments. Values are things you act on. If there's a price to pay, you pay it. Sentiments are—they're like visitation rights to values. You talk it up, you sound impressive, but before matters get messy, I'm out of there.

JOANNA: It's so hard, isn't it?

ELLIOT: Maybe talk helps.

JOANNA: Elliot, the reason you hate those words I say—"don't let it get to you," "don't get upset"? They are warnings, those words. "Piece of cake" means "keep your distance, thank you kindly." I have a secret life, Elliot, that I don't know the secret to, but I do know it is there and I'm not telling. Your thoughtfulness, Elliot. What I was attacking was that your thoughtfulness confounds me. It terrifies me because I wonder, what does this man want from me? What in the world does he want from me? Stop knocking at my door! No one is home. You stop knocking at my door—all right? And if you do, I will stop saying "piece of cake." Well? (*Pause.*) Can we shake on that?

(*Pause.*)

ELLIOT: I don't know what else to do. I have to keep knocking. I love you, Joanna. Are you there? . . . are you there? . . .

JOANNA: . . . I'm thinking.

BLACKOUT

Selected Plays & Screenplays
Available from Grove Weidenfeld

___ GUERN	0-8021-5122-1	Arrabal, Fernando GUERNICA AND OTHER PLAYS	$17.50
___ ABSURD	0-8021-3157-3	Ayckbourn, Alan THREE PLAYS (Absurd Person Singular; Absent Friends; Bedroom Farce)	$9.95
___ CASCA	0-8021-5099-3	Beckett, Samuel CASCANDO	$8.95
___ ENDGA	0-8021-5024-1	Beckett, Samuel ENDGAME and ACT WITHOUT WORDS	$4.95
___ ENDS	0-8021-5046-2	Beckett, Samuel ENDS AND ODDS	$8.95
___ KRAPP	0-8021-5134-5	Beckett, Samuel KRAPP'S LAST TAPE	$7.95
___ GODOT	0-8021-3034-8	Beckett, Samuel WAITING FOR GODOT	$5.95
___ BEHAN	0-8021-3070-4	Behan, Brendan THE COMPLETE PLAYS (The Hostage; The Quare Fellow; Richard's Cork Leg)	$9.95
___ KVETC	0-8021-3001-1	Berkoff, Steven KVETCH and ACAPULCO	$6.95
___ BAAL	0-8021-3159-X	Brecht, Bertolt BAAL, A MAN'S A MAN, and THE ELEPHANT CALF	$8.95
___ CAUCA	0-8021-5146-9	Brecht, Bertolt THE CAUCASIAN CHALK CIRCLE	$5.95
___ GALIL	0-8021-3059-3	Brecht, Bertolt GALILEO	$5.95
___ GOOD	0-8021-5148-5	Brecht, Bertolt THE GOOD WOMAN OF SETZUAN	$4.50
___ JUNGL	0-8021-5149-3	Brecht, Bertolt THE JUNGLE OF THE CITIES	$9.95
___ 3PENNY	0-8021-5039-X	Brecht, Bertolt THREEPENNY OPERA	$4.95
___ CHERR	0-8021-3002-X	Chekhov, Anton THE CHERRY ORCHARD	$8.95
___ NINE	0-8021-5032-2	Clurman, Harold (ed.) NINE PLAYS OF THE MODERN THEATRE (Waiting for Godot; The Visit; Tango; The Caucasian Chalk Circle; The Balcony; Rhinoceros; American Buffalo; The Birthday Party; Rosencrantz & Guildenstern Are Dead)	$16.95
___ 3BYCOW	0-8021-5108-6	Coward, Noel THREE PLAYS (Private Lives; Hay Fever; Blithe Spirit)	$9.95
___ LAUGH	0-8021-3130-1	Durang, Christopher LAUGHING WILD and BABY WITH THE BATHWATER	$7.95
___ BETBOO	0-394-62347-9	Durang, Christopher THE MARRIAGE OF BETTE AND BOO	$7.95
___ PHYSI	0-8021-5088-8	Durrenmatt, Friedrich THE PHYSICISTS	$6.95
___ COUSI	0-8021-3152-2	Foote, Horton COUSINS and THE DEATH OF PAPA	$8.95
___ TOKILL	0-8021-3125-5	Foote, Horton TO KILL A MOCKINGBIRD, TRIP TO BOUNTIFUL, TENDER MERCIES	$10.95
___ RAPPA	0-8021-3044-5	Gardner, Herb I'M NOT RAPPAPORT	$7.95
___ BALCO	0-8021-5034-9	Genet, Jean THE BALCONY	$8.95
___ EASTE	0-8021-3174-3	Greenberg, Richard EASTERN STANDARD	$9.95
___ SECRE	0-8021-3175-1	Hare, David THE SECRET RAPTURE	$8.95
___ LARGO	0-8021-5163-9	Havel, Vaclav LARGO DESOLATO	$7.95
___ TEMPT	0-8021-3100-X	Havel, Vaclav TEMPTATION	$9.95
___ INGE	0-8021-5065-9	Inge, William FOUR PLAYS (Come Back Little Sheba; Picnic; Bus Stop; The Dark At the Top of the Stairs)	$9.95
___ BALD	0-8021-3079-8	Ionesco, Eugene FOUR PLAYS (Bald Soprano; The Lesson; Jack or Submission; The Chairs)	$8.95
___ RHINO	0-8021-3098-4	Ionesco, Eugene RHINOCEROS AND OTHER PLAYS	$7.95
___ EXITKI	0-8021-5110-8	Ionesco, Eugene THREE PLAYS (Exit the King; The Killer; Macbett)	$12.95
___ UBUPLA	0-8021-5010-1	Jarry, Alfred THE UBU PLAYS	$9.95
___ AUREV	0-8021-3114-X	Malle, Louis AU REVOIR LES ENFANTS	$6.95
___ 5TV	0-8021-3171-9	Mamet, David FIVE TELEVISION PLAYS	$12.95
___ GLENG	0-8021-3091-7	Mamet, David GLENGARRY GLEN ROSS	$6.95
___ GAMES	0-8021-3028-3	Mamet, David HOUSE OF GAMES	$5.95
___ LIFETH	0-8021-5067-5	Mamet, David A LIFE IN THE THEATRE	$9.95

Selections from Grove Weidenfeld (continued)

____ SPEED	0-8021-3046-1	Mamet, David SPEED-THE-PLOW	$7.95
____ CLOCK	0-8021-3127-1	Miller, Arthur THE AMERICAN CLOCK and THE ARCHBISHOP'S CEILING	$8.95
____ DANGER	0-8021-5176-0	Miller, Arthur DANGER: MEMORY	$5.95
____ ODETS	0-8021-5060-8	Odets, Clifford SIX PLAYS (Waiting for Lefty; Awake and Sing; Golden Boy; Rocket to the Moon; Till the Day I Die; Paradise Lost)	$10.95
____ ORTON	0-8021-3039-9	Orton, Joe THE COMPLETE PLAYS (The Ruffian on the Stairs; The Good and Faithful Servant; The Erpingham Camp; Funeral Games; Loot; What the Butler Saw; Entertaining Mr. Sloane)	$10.95
____ CARET	0-8021-5087-X	Pinter, Harold THE CARETAKER and THE DUMB WAITER	$7.95
____ MOUNT	0-8021-3168-9	Pinter, Harold MOUNTAIN LANGUAGE	$6.95
____ PROUS	0-8021-5191-4	Pinter, Harold THE PROUST SCREENPLAY	$3.95
____ ELEPHM	0-8021-3041-0	Pomerance, Bernard THE ELEPHANT MAN	$6.95
____ HURLY	0-8021-5097-7	Rabe, David HURLYBURLY	$7.95
____ BOOM	0-8021-5194-9	Rabe, David IN THE BOOM BOOM ROOM	$8.95
____ AUNT	0-8021-5103-5	Shawn, Wallace AUNT DAN AND LEMON	$8.95
____ ANDRE	0-8021-3063-1	Shawn, Wallace MY DINNER WITH ANDRE	$7.95
____ EVERY	0-8021-5045-4	Stoppard, Tom EVERY GOOD BOY DESERVES FAVOR and PROFESSIONAL FOUL	$3.95
____ REAL	0-8021-5205-8	Stoppard, Tom THE REAL INSPECTOR HOUND and AFTER MARGRITE	$7.95
____ ROSEN	0-8021-3033-X	Stoppard, Tom ROSENCRANTZ & GUILDENSTERN ARE DEAD	$6.95
____ TRAVE	0-8021-5089-6	Stoppard, Tom TRAVESTIES	$4.95
____ NOPLAY	0-8021-5206-6	Waley, Arthur (trans.) NO PLAYS OF JAPAN	$9.95
____ COLOR	0-8021-3048-8	Wolfe, George C. THE COLORED MUSEUM	$7.95

TO ORDER DIRECTLY FROM GROVE WEIDENFELD:

YES! Please send me the books selected above.

Telephone orders—credit card only: 1-800-937-5557.

Mail orders: Please include $1.50 postage and handling, plus $.50 for each additional book, or credit card information requested below.

Send to: Grove Weidenfeld
IPS
1113 Heil Quaker Boulevard
P.O. Box 7001
La Vergne, TN 37086-7001

☐ I have enclosed $_____ (check or money order only)

☐ Please charge my Visa/MasterCard card account (circle one).

Card Number_____

Expiration Date_____

Signature_____

Name_____

Address_____ Apt. _____

City_____ State _____ Zip _____

Please allow 4–6 weeks for delivery.
Please note that prices are subject to change without notice.
For additional information, catalogues or bulk sales inquiries, please call 1-800-937-5557.   ADCD